CW00422202

THE

AFTERMATH

THE ULTIMATE SURVIVAL

Elsie Frederick

BALBOA.PRESS

A DIVISION OF HAY HOUSE

Balboa Press books may be ordered through booksellers or by contacting:

Balboa Press
A Division of Hay House
1663 Liberty Drive
Bloomington, IN 47403
www.balboapress.co.uk
UK TFN: 0800 0148647 (Toll Free inside the UK)
UK Local: 02036 956325 (+44 20 3695 6325 from outside the UK)

Because of the dynamic nature of the Internet, any web addresses or
links contained in this book may have changed since publication and
may no longer be valid. The views expressed in this work are solely those
of the author and do not necessarily reflect the views of the publisher,
and the publisher hereby disclaims any responsibility for them.

The author of this book does not dispense medical advice or prescribe the use
of any technique as a form of treatment for physical, emotional, or medical
problems without the advice of a physician, either directly or indirectly. The
intent of the author is only to offer information of a general nature to help
you in your quest for emotional and spiritual well-being. In the event you use
any of the information in this book for yourself, which is your constitutional
right, the author and the publisher assume no responsibility for your actions.

Any people depicted in stock imagery provided by Getty Images are
models, and such images are being used for illustrative purposes only.
Certain stock imagery © Getty Images.

Print information available on the last page.

ISBN: 978-1-9822-8244-8 (sc)
ISBN: 978-1-9822-8245-5 (e)

Balboa Press rev. date: 10/19/2020

CONTENTS

JANUARY 2020

I have not looked at my book for some years now. It has just sat untouched on my computer and so much has changed since I last wrote. It is because the law on Organ Donation is about to change this year in 2020 that I have picked up my computer mouse to write the second part of the story. It will be assumed now that, unless you opt out, then your organs can be used for transplantation, long overdue in my opinion, but a controversial subject, nevertheless.

So, I need to bring my tale up to date. Originally, I started to write this story as a diary, a catharsis, to help me get through those difficult and dark days of George's serious health issues. Do not get me wrong, we had some terrible times with George's medical history, but we also had a very good life together most of the time. You have to take the rough with the smooth in any life and like your marriage vows state, for richer or poorer, for better or worse, in sickness and in health.

Well, we had some definitely poorer and worse days, from having a £750,000 overdraft in 1990, with 4 kids at home, school fees to pay, a major recession, properties for sale when the market was dead and a garage full of cars when nobody could afford to buy them. But somehow we survived. We worked hard, kept our heads down and got through it and came out on the other side.

We had some richer days when the property market picked up. We had bought at the right price, developed some beautiful barn conversions and then sold them at a decent profit. We developed Top Farm, Seven Spouts Farm and Lowes Farm. Quite an achievement taking George's medical history into consideration..

We had some wonderful and better times, we were so fortunate to be able to travel, holiday, cruise whenever and wherever we wanted; go motor racing, the British Grand Prix, Monaco and Indianapolis, Goodwood, British Racing Drivers Club. I am just so grateful to have had those opportunities.

In sickness, George continued with medical blips for a few years but then encountered some major ones too, but for the first 10 years following his transplant we had a fairly healthy time. My health has always been surprisingly good. As I get older, I have some arthritic joints but nothing bad enough to stop me yet!

2008 / 2009

My story moves somewhat from being a tale of how we lived through a heart transplant, if that isn't a subject so monumental on its' own. The ensuing years bring me onto the seriousness and devastation of the impact of Stroke and Dementia. As we now have an aging population, these are conditions that have become more prevalent in our society. It now becomes a story of how we dealt with these conditions, the devastation, how to live with the aftermath, the need for understanding and support from family and friends.

In 2008 we bought yet another property development in a nearby village. Much to my distress, we sold my beloved Lowes House and moved to the complete antithesis of a Georgian country house. The Key House is much older; fifteenth century, and the oldest house in the village. Instead of lovely views of fields and the river, we lived on the main road with lots of traffic noise which irritated me beyond belief. Instead of big, south facing, sash windows letting in the sun, we had north facing, little leaded glass panes, instead of lovely airy high-ceilinged rooms, we had low beamed ceilings on which anyone approaching 6 feet tall would, without due care, render themselves unconscious. I really did not want George to do another conversion, but he was determined and with that same single-minded obstinacy, set about bringing the old house back to life. It needed total renovation, both inside and out, a huge undertaking which I was convinced was a step too far, too much work, too much stress dealing with planners and conservation officers. We did not need to do it, but George said he had one more project in him. The rationale behind the financing this "final project" was that, as there was a very long garden to the rear of the house, half of the orchard area had outline planning permission to build several houses using an entrance already on the plans at the bottom of the land. This meant that the profit from the sale of this land would fund the renovation. So, as usual, I went along with the plan as it was just not worth the grief to argue.

To keep myself sane and fulfil a lifetime dream, the year previously, I had decided to do a university degree in Interior Design. I had always wanted to do this and as I had been doing the interiors of all our barn conversions informally for the past 20 years, it was formalizing what I already had done by the seat of my pants but without proper training. I knew I was going to be enlightened and inspired and that it was the right time to do something for me. My Dad would be proud of me as I had turned down my university place at age 18 because I wanted to go straight from school to do the management training course at John Lewis. As Dad said," better late than never, kid". I needed to throw my energies into something entirely different. (I graduated in July 2012 with a BA Hons degree, so despite everything I am immensely proud of myself).

My predictions were correct, the strain was too much, another battle with planners and building inspectors took its' toll on George. We had not yet sold Lowes House and were still living there but had completed the purchase of The Key House with a bridging loan secured on Lowes House. George was very fired up with enthusiasm for this project, it gave him, briefly, a new purpose to life, something to get his teeth into. We got our old team of builders back together, had meetings with all the authorities involved, and a full-on major renovation project got underway. George was up with the lark and off to be with the team when they started at 8am. One Monday, in early September, Woody, our foreman, rang me to say he had sent George home as he was not feeling well. He just wanted to make sure I was at home. George duly arrived about 10 minutes later, ashen faced, shaking all over, his body totally out of control. Heaven knows how he had driven back home. I got him into bed still shaking. He said he was freezing cold, so I thought at first he was brewing a dose of flu and put a hot water bottle in bed with him and wrapped him up warm. I phoned the emergency services as I quickly recognised that this was something much more serious. His symptoms were more like the ones he had when he was in Florida where he had, somehow, contracted septicaemia. I was very concerned obviously. The ambulance crew arrived quickly and diagnosed George with a "Rigor", a serious infection and sky-high temperature. Of course, I had made him as warm as possible, but in reality, I should have put him in a tepid bath to bring his temperature down! I had done exactly the opposite of what I should have done. Oh, sometimes I wish I had more medical knowledge. Anyway, he was taken straight to our local hospital and admitted. Put on an antibiotic drip and fluids, he was there for several days to stabilize him.

On the following Friday, I had arranged to take Mum and Dad to Birmingham Airport to go on a river cruise in Germany. The evening before, whilst I was visiting George, the doctor told him that, all being well, he would be discharged the following day, so I arranged to pick him up after taking my parents to the airport. I dropped Mum and Dad off and as I was about to leave Birmingham airport, I rang George from the car park, who said that he was about to go in the shower. I said I would be about an hour and a half as I was going to The Key House first to pay the guys before getting George home, then all the jobs would be finished, and I could devote the time to make sure George was ok for the weekend.

I arrived at the Key House about 40 minutes later and my mobile phone was ringing as I went up the drive. It was in the days before mobiles connect to cars by Bluetooth; I could see it was Georges number on the phone screen, but I ignored it whilst manoeuvring to park between the builders van, cement mixers and a delivery lorry. As soon as I was parked up, I rang him back. A strange voice answered the phone and introduced himself as the doctor on duty. He wanted me to get to the hospital immediately as George had, apparently, collapsed in the shower, was found on the floor and had suffered a major stroke. What? I had only spoken to him 40 minutes earlier when he sounded fine, was packed and ready to be discharged other than getting in the shower. I said that I was on my way. Grabbed the cheque book, found Woody up in the roof, explained quickly that I had to get to the hospital asap and gave him a signed blank cheque. "Please sort out the wages for the guys, Woody, and let me know later how much you've spent!" That is trust for you. Woody has always been the best builder and plasterer, honest as the day is long and does a great job. Not too many like him around!!

I raced to the hospital, wondering what on earth I

was going to find. My heart sank into my boots. Oh no, not again, I groaned inside. After years of dealing with heart attacks and transplants, I was quite au fait with the associated medical terminology, pill regimes etc. but I had no idea about strokes. Completely at sea here, what does all this mean? How bad? Whatever next would we have to deal with?

I arrived; George was on a hospital trolley bed in the ward waiting to be transferred to the stroke unit. A brain CT scan had been ordered and another barrage of blood tests to be done. George took one look at me and cried; tears streamed down his face. He could not move his arms or legs; worse, he could not speak. Not a word. Not even a sound. Oh, the tears really got to me. All the illnesses, heart disease, septicaemia, infections, surgeries over all those years, never had I seen him cry. The fear in his eyes was dreadful to see. I cried too. "come on George", I said," we've got through some stuff before, we will get through this too. Let's get you sorted out, let's get these tests done and find out what we are dealing with." How I sounded so calm, I don't know? As usual when faced with a crisis, I go into Mrs Super-Efficient mode, take control, be positive, be upbeat, although I was terrified and no idea what I was doing. So, we got through the tests, got the blood tests done, got him into the Stroke ward and waited. I rang John and Ann to tell them that their dad had suffered a Stroke, and could they come and visit as soon as possible. So, we were back in the same scenario as we were in 1997. Back to square 1. Just bought a new building renovation project with a major medical condition to handle at the same time. It was almost like déjà vu. Different project, different medical condition but back to being a whirling dervish, nurse, building project manager, planners to deal with, team of builders to control, kids, although grown-ups now, and committed to a degree course.

Not again. Words failed me.

We soon found out that he had a clot in his brain; thank goodness it wasn't a bleed, which meant another pill regime, conversations ensued between the Stroke Team and Harefield as what pills were and were not compatible with the pills he was already on. I thought that he would rattle if he took any more tablets but, as with everything, you get used to it and just get on and deal with it. The stroke left him unable to speak for several weeks but "bloody minded" as ever, he was determined to get better His movement came back, but slowly. His speech took much longer to return, and we had to get a speech therapist to help. He knew what he wanted to say but the words would not come out right, upside down and inside out. I described it to him as the brain is like a library. All the books are in precise order and catalogued. When a stroke happens it's like an earthquake in the brain and all the books are shaken off the shelves. The books are all still there but not in the right order, they are in a heap on the floor and it takes much longer to locate the book you are looking for. George would look me straight in the eyes then look to the door, he was trying to get me to guess what he wanted and got really agitated as I had no clue, I tried coffee, no, water, no, do you need the loo, no, do you need a nurse, no. It was a guessing game and I was not much good at it. It was so frustrating for him. One day Ann and I were sitting at the bottom of George's bed, just chatting away about this and that, just inconsequential conversation. George was getting tired, but we had not noticed. He got so aggravated, and with a monumental effort, said "bugger off". It didn't quite come out right, but we certainly got the meaning. We both laughed, and almost cried with emotion and with relief as they were the first words he had said in 3 weeks.

During this time, I went to see Woody and explained the situation. We were at a point when we were waiting for planning consents to come through, so it was a good time to let the team go and do other jobs till we were ready to start again. It was late October and winter was starting so we laid everyone off till after Christmas. That gave me time to concentrate on getting George back to as good health as possible

The therapy we had was not really very much use but we did get George to go for a walk every day to strengthen his leg muscles, which had weakened drastically. The problem was that he could not remember where he lived, could not speak well enough to ask, and he kept getting lost. I wrote a note to put in his coat pocket. I said to him "if you get lost just hand somebody this note". On it, a bit like Paddington Bear's brown label, it said "My name is George, I've had a stroke, please return me to my wife at Lowes House etc and my wife's phone number is …." Several times complete strangers put him into their cars and brought him home. Oh, what another major stress, strain and worry. I had known all along that The Key House project was a step too far but even if I had objected at the time, George would have gone ahead anyway!!!

As before, we got through it together but as George's speech returned, so did his bad temper. As in previous chapters, this was due in part to frustration with himself, he could see that I was fit and healthy and there was a type of envy about that. His balance was not good; I had to help him have a shower as he was scared of falling, he became very thin with huge muscle wastage and he was permanently tired. His temper was vitriolic; he would fly off the handle at the slightest thing. He was very rude and insulting to me, so hurtful when I was the one person doing everything for him, but I tried ridiculously hard to let it go over my head. When friends said to me that they didn't know how I put up with the insults and hurtful words, I just used to say, "it goes in one ear and out the other side, George obviously thinks I have no brain so there is nothing to stop it". Of course it hurt but what could I do? There was no point in arguing; it just made things worse. I developed a skin as thick as an elephant.

I had my girlfriends who were lifesavers; I had my studying which I was able to throw myself into during the afternoons when George had gone to bed to rest and in the early hours when I couldn't sleep, and I had the Doghouse Ladies. I have not mentioned them yet in this tale, but the real title is "The Women's Motor Racing Associates Club". A very famous group of Ladies, prestigious in the world of motor sport, originally set up in the 1950's by the F1 drivers wives, as a self-help group; it developed and evolved, as did motor sport, eventually becoming a group of friends involved with motor racing, providing support to each other in times of difficulty and accidents, which then developed by inviting any lady associated with motor sport, drivers, marshals, mechanics, sponsors, team managers, making them eligible to become members. We did a lot of fundraising for charities associated with motor sport. I was hugely honoured to be asked to join back in 2000, then voted to be treasurer / secretary, finally becoming chairman in 2009. At present (2020) we are about 120 strong, a bunch of lovely, strong, formidable ladies I am so proud to be able to call friends. We worked hard to raise lots of money for worthwhile causes, drawing on our contacts and considerable abilities, whilst having a great deal of fun and laughter. A fair few glass of wine were consumed as well! Sadly, through the passage of time and our age, a lot of the original ladies have now passed away. Their husbands were legends on the racetrack and these ladies supported them on and off the pit wall through their early days of racing. It isn't the same these days, sponsorship, safety regulations, insurances make it a much safer sport than in the past. The wives no longer sit on the pit wall with a stopwatch, baby tucked under their arms, timing laps, then making sandwiches and pots of tea for the teams of mechanics in caravans. It is another world now. Fortunately, much safer and fatalities, thankfully scarce, but big business has taken it over and, whilst it is still exciting, not the sport it used to be.

Without my distractions and support though, I'm not sure how I would have coped.

As before, when George went through the transplant phase, the carer, i.e.me, becomes isolated; difficult for others to understand what you are going through. So, my distractions became immensely important. My children were so aware of what I was going through as well as the struggles that George was dealing with, they were so supportive of us both. Ann and John, however, in my opinion, spent a lot of time in total denial of the seriousness of the situation and told me more than once that I was making a crisis out of a drama. They did not live with George: I did. They came to visit, Ann more infrequently as she lived south of London, John more often as he lived locally, when George would put on a huge show of happiness and effort to see them, but they never saw the tired, irritable, angry and frustrated man that he became after they left. I asked John on one occasion if he and David would tidy up George's garage and get everything in order, nuts, bolts, screws, and get rid of the bits of paper and the rubbish. It was a chaotic mess. Drill bits, lawn mowers; all sorts of stuff. "Please make some sense of it for me please guys" John thought I was dreadful actually asking him to do something like that. "Dad likes to put his garage in order himself, he would think I was interfering" John said. He didn't understand that George could not do it, he couldn't even start to think how to put it back in order, His brain wasn't yet reprogrammed to think. Everything had to be done for him, If I put a meal in front of him, he would just look at it till I picked up his knife and fork for him and put them in his hands. He just had no power of independent thought.

Xmas was a bit of a turning point for him. He enjoyed it, having everyone around, laughed at granddaughter Ruby's antics. At 11, she was a typically, normal girl, full of cheek and fun. George could only cope with her, however, for a short while; he was not strong enough to cope with anything for long, but his speech had become more improved and he could at least join in.

As soon as Xmas and New Year was over, I insisted we had a holiday, a break before he started work again, some warm sun and some well-earned rest. A Caribbean cruise was just what was needed, and we had a lovely 2 weeks away. George always enjoyed going on holiday but towards the end he started to get itchy feet about the Key House project. So, as soon as we returned the team was reassembled, and we set back to work. George, much to his disgust, was not allowed to drive following his stroke so I would drive him there in the morning and bring him home at lunchtime. He could only cope for a few hours and the weather was very cold too. I had many private meetings with Woody and basically we made most of the decisions about the project, which infuriated George as he wanted to be the driving force; he just couldn't make the right decisions, his brain capacity was simply not up to it. He fell out with the planners, the conservation officer, pretty much everyone, and me in particular, but never Woody. Anyone who crossed him or disagreed with him got the brunt of his temper. I had to become co-project manager, designing all the fixtures and fittings. Whilst choosing the kitchen we had a monumental argument about an Aga. I wanted one and George did not. I argued that I had cooked on an Aga for nigh on 20 years and asked him when he had last cooked a meal? He won that one though, as he went and ordered a gas oven range whilst I was out one day choosing bathroom fittings and when I arrived the following day, the range had been delivered. There wasn't much point in arguing. I know which arguments to pick and this wasn't one of them. The following week, I drove George out to a marble supplier near Matlock to choose work surfaces. In all the years we had been together, we had argued about many things; on this occasion we looked at dozens of huge slabs of beautiful marble and then suddenly, we both chose the same one. We laughed so much on the way home about actually agreeing on something, we opened a bottle of champagne that evening to celebrate. Our marriage had always been a lively one. Both very alpha characters, both like to have the upper hand and both extraordinarily strong willed. Inevitably it was full of ups and downs but never ever boring.

And so, during the spring of 2009, the renovation of the interior of The Key House progressed. I had an accident, slipping on wet grass in the paddock at Lowes House, I was chasing after the dog who was barking at a poor little hedgehog and I was trying to save the poor little creature who was curled into a tight ball whilst the dog was running round and round. I fell and badly hurt my right knee. Oh, it swelled up like a football and made it difficult to walk and drive. Very fortunately George had managed to persuade the doctors to allow him to drive again, much to my disagreement as half the time he did not know where he was going, but at least one of us could drive.

Bless his heart, my lovely friend Peter, mentioned many times before in this book, looked at my knee and said it required surgery and that he would do it. Gave me a date at the beginning of September. George thought this was wonderful. Elsie would be out of action for a week or 2 so booked the removal firm to move us from Lowes House into The Key House. I was furious, how was I supposed to pack up this huge house and move when I could barely walk. I questioned his powers of reason, but he just did not get it, he said that the removal firm would do it all. I knew they certainly would not. We hadn't sold Lowes House, we didn't have to move in a mad hurry, what was all the rush. I didn't want to move there at all. I'd much rather have stayed at Lowes House, finished the exterior renovation of the Key House and sold it. But no. What George wanted, George did and got. No discussion, argument or compromise.

This is when I really started to question George's capabilities, his power of reason, his inconsistences, he was just doing some irrational things. A few days later a van arrived outside the house, from one of the Auction Houses in town. George had asked them to collect a valuable painting, an oak dresser and some other items of furniture. What! Where did that come from in his brain. Oh, a monumental standoff ensued. George argued that it was his furniture and therefore could do what he liked. He said they would not go into the new house. I argued that they would and anyway we had not sold Lowes House and it was far from certain that we would sell it. In the end a compromise was reached, and they took the oak dresser. It broke my heart. It was a beautiful piece of furniture and housed all our dinner service and cut glass, which ended up in piles on the dining room floor. I rang a friend who agreed to look after the painting and a statue until agreement was reached.

In hindsight, and wouldn't it be wonderful if we had that ability, these were the first signs that, following George's Stroke 10 months previously, were the tell-tale signs of the beginnings of Vascular Dementia, what I would do to have had that knowledge then. So much of what happened later may have been prevented.

Hindsight!

But George had his way. He used to accuse me of making him feel ill if I argued with him, just like before, the emotional blackmail, the coercive control. So, I tried not to, it is very hard when he is doing things that really you

15

do not want to do but agree to for fear of being accused of making him ill.

August saw Georges 65th birthday. He wanted to go on a Windstar cruise again so off we went. We both loved that ship with its sails, small and intimate, not like the monster ships with thousands of people and it was the third time we had sailed with them. We visited, amongst many other places, Sicily. Such a beautiful island. The first time we visited was in 1998 on the first cruise we had ever done. Leaving the ship, that first time, we travelled to Taormina, a particular historic site on the other side of the island. On that occasion, as mentioned earlier in the book, the atrocious weather caused a monumental tragedy, a huge storm and torrential downpour, caused a landslide, bringing earth and rocks down the mountain side, collapsing the motorway in its' path and burying the coastal villages. Such a disaster; people's homes were destroyed in the landslide; some sadly lost their lives. It was truly dreadful to be caught up in it. We managed, with the help of a somewhat demented taxi driver, who ignored all the warning signs and diversions to get us back to the ship. So, on our second visit to Taormina I was determined to get photographs and see what I had missed on the first trip. I was so busy snapping away, I twisted round to get a better angle and – ouch, as I turned, I felt my knee tear. The pain was jaw dropping. I was rooted to the spot and I couldn't move. Rendered speechless, and that never happens, as my friends would verify, I didn't know how to move; the pain was shooting right through my body. I had arranged to meet George at 2pm, together with 2 other people with whom we had arranged to share a taxi, at the edge of the village as the main street was a pedestrian only area. I am still not sure how I got back to the meeting place. I was in agony and I literally hopped from one shop door front to the next having to rest and gather myself for the next hop. I was staggering and think that everyone watching me, probably thought I was drunk. Literally holding myself up in doorways, I was obviously in difficulty, but no one came to my rescue. I could hear George shouting my name at the end of the street, but he couldn't see me. Eventually, the 2 lovely guys, our taxi and cruise buddies, came to find me and helped me to the car. Well that scuppered my fun on the rest of the cruise. I dosed myself with as many paracetamols as possible, could barely walk and knew the knee was in dire need of the operation. It could not be put off any longer.

Early in September I was summoned for surgery. The same day the removal van had been arranged. There are no words I can say here to describe how I felt. Was George taking me to the hospital? No. After all the years I had driven him to and from hospitals, doctors, appointments! Where was the husband to care and look after me when I needed him? One of my lovely friends volunteered to take me from Lowes House to the hospital and so off I went first thing in the morning. Later that day, with crutches and an immense bandage around my knee, feeling somewhat bruised and battered and in a lot of discomfort, she collected me and returned me to my new home, The Key House. As I had known what would happen, the removal people had packed dozens of boxes and moved them, but not unpacked them. The bed was up in the bedroom but not made up, the clothes were all in cardboard wardrobe carriers but not put away in the wardrobes! It was chaotic, things in wrong rooms, the kitchen was mayhem. It was a disaster. All I wanted to do was run away and cry, but I could not run; I could not even walk.

As ever, somehow, we gradually got through it, got the house up and running, unpacked and liveable in. I needed to get fit as soon as possible. It would be my 60th birthday in November and I was determined to wear high heels and dance. By the look of my knee, that was going to be a tall order. Every day I walked a little bit further, every day I got a bit more used to the house, every day I hated the noise from the main road and the aircraft taking off overhead. Every day I missed Lowes House more and more. Once our new house was sorted and I was allowed to drive again, I would go up to Lowes House and just look at what we had left. It was up for sale but so far no one had made an offer despite many viewings. I was so very unhappy at that point. I was living somewhere I did not want to be, with a husband who was increasingly difficult, irrational and bad tempered, everything in the world that was wrong was my fault. I was really confused about how my life was going to pan out in the future. I just could not see how it could get any better. I was right, the next three years got increasingly worse.

My 60th birthday party was, however, a triumph. I wore shoes with heels (I had flat comfy ones under the table though). I'd booked the upstairs function suite at the our favourite hostelry, the owners were great friends, 60 guests, all my family, my daughter had returned from her stay in Australia, my brother had returned from New Zealand so the whole gang was there, and my best friends, a great singer, fabulous dinner and shed loads of wine. It was a great night. I had bought an incredible vintage "flapper" dress, covered in beads. It weighed a ton, but it was a showstopper. I needed that, as inside my confidence was rock bottom, I was not in a happy place and I was 60!!! Anyway, it was a brilliant party and I enjoyed every minute of it.

2010

As I said in the previous chapter, I was beginning to question George's decision-making abilities. Looking back as I write this account, I realise that I did not recognise the symptom of dementia because the progression was so slow. I put everything down to the transplant, the stroke, the associated pill regime, the stress of the projects, anything other than recognising that it was dementia, but his temper did not improve, it just got worse. The only times that George was in good humour was when we were on holiday. It got him away from the routine and so I planned to take him away as much as possible.

I enjoyed those respite periods too. It gave my poor knee time to recover and getting out into the sunshine always helped. We had a lovely week in a great hotel in Tenerife in March, and in June we went on a fantastic Greek Island Cruise. I had always wanted to go to Greece, the history, the beauty, the culture, oh it was amazing. We went on a tiny ship, about 30 of us, it was like having your own personal yacht. How fab was that? George loved it, regaling the stories of his racing days and his heart transplant. He had a captive audience who were genuinely interested. Our fellow shipmates were a lovely group of people, the islands were lovely, the weather delightful, I wished that it could go on and on. Such a lovely holiday.

Unfortunately, at Athens airport on the way home, I had a catastrophe. We had a 4 hour wait for our flight, so we went to the hotel opposite the departure terminal, had a swim, a massage, hair do and lunch. After a very relaxing morning, I went across the tarmac car park in order to cross the road into the airport to see if it was time to check in. However, I did it, I will never know, but I tripped over, went down like a plank, hit my chin first and then grazed the whole of my face. I just lay on the ground, too stunned to move. Several people rushed to help me get up, but the hotel manager took charge. He phoned for an ambulance which took me to the airport medical centre. George, meanwhile, was sitting, oblivious to my plight, in the hotel lounge. I had to get the manager to find George to inform him of where I was. He was driven up to the medical centre where I was being examined by a doctor. They concluded that despite my facial injuries, my jaw and teeth were not broken and so deemed that I was well enough to fly. Read into that – they wanted me out of the country pdq before I could cause any problems with a dangerous uneven tarmac driveway! The manager kindly escorted us and the luggage to the check in desk and wished us well. I looked like I had been hit by a bus, bleeding, grazed, bruised and in shock. George asked the girl at the check in desk to get him disabled help to the flight, which I had already booked anyway. So, the wheelchair duly arrived but with no one to help, so I, looking as if I was on the point of collapse and needed the wheelchair myself, pushed him through security and passport control to the boarding gate. The air hostess on the flight could not believe what she was seeing and immediately took control. Settled George into his seat then took me off to a different part of the plane and made me lie down, brought me pillows and blankets, some paracetamol and a cup of tea. I slept the whole flight home. I drove home from the airport, I'm still not sure how, and George never mentioned my face or even asked how I was. He was only concerned about himself, getting home safely and what was for dinner that night. I ordered a Chinese take away to be delivered!!! After 2 weeks away and with no food in the house, looking like I had been in a tram smash, did George honestly think I was capable of going shopping and cooking? Such a shame as the holiday had been so wonderful. I went to the doctors as soon as I could get an appointment, was sent for x rays which thankfully revealed no broken jaw, but that I had fractured the roots of my front 4 top teeth. This resulted in long, and immensely expensive dental reconstruction work over the next 18 months. Amazing isn't it that George could get so much medical treatment in Florida on the travel insurance but injury to teeth are not covered!

It took several weeks to recover and heal my face, I went from black and blue to a gentle shade of greenish yellow, I had gouged a deep lump out of my cheek which grew a massive scab, swollen cheeks; I've looked better; Quasimodo looked better!!!

The first weekend in September was a brilliant one for George. His famous racing car which had been bought as a chassis by a lovely guy some years before, had been lovingly restored and at the Historic Car Race Meeting weekend at Donington Park Circuit, it was being raced by one of George's oldest racing friends, Dougie. Along with Robert and Lindsay, who had a Hospitality Suite for the weekend, we watched Dougie race, had lots of friends visit and we entertained and partied all weekend.

A week later we went off on holiday again. George was on good form from the previous weekend and in good humour, despite the slow but noticeable decline in his health. This time we went on a Seabourn Cruise, total luxury, waited on hand and foot. This time it was to the Mediterranean. As usual, I did all the booking, George used to leave all the logistics to me and this time I played a blinder and excelled myself. The times we had been to the South of France are too many to remember but suffice to say we knew the area well. The cruise was departing from Monaco Harbour and the flights were to Nice, returning from Barcelona a week later. I phoned our racing friends who lived in Beaulieu, on the Cote d' Azur, to say we would be in Nice on September 11th, were they free to meet for lunch? Oh joy, yes, they were. Our flight arrived about 10.30am. To get to Monaco takes about 45 minutes to drive but we didn't have a car. We could catch the bus from the airport into Nice then get the train to Monaco, which would take about an hour and a half. We could get a taxi from the airport straight to Monaco for about £100 or … we could take the Monaco Heli Air Helicopter service which takes about 15 minutes maximum, then they provide a taxi free of charge from the heliport to anywhere in the city. The times George and I had watched racing drivers, film stars, celebrities and royalty use the helicopter. George's health was not great and so I booked it. I knew it would be a once in a lifetime chance and that George would love it. I kept it a total secret and it wasn't until we were on the flight that George suddenly asked, "how are we getting from Nice to Monaco?" I fobbed him off with the bus, train and taxi option and I saw his face fall. How would he ever manage all that and with a wheelchair? It wasn't until we had landed, collected our luggage and were making our way out of the terminal when I said to him," you know you always said that one day you'd like to fly into Monaco by helicopter, like the rich and famous? Well today is the day". He beamed. Oh, good job, well done me. That scored many, much needed, Brownie points. So, like celebrities, we flew into Monaco by Heli Air, were taken by a sleek black Mercedes limo to the Monaco Yacht Club for lunch with 4 lovely friends. What a fabulous start to the holiday. Absolutely stunning, but only a 10 minute flight. The French Riviera and coastline is spectacular viewed from a boat but from the air it was breath-taking. Even now I still pinch myself to think that I was so privileged to witness that and be able to just glimpse the world of the glitterati. Not a life I would want to live but wonderful just to have the experience for a snapshot moment. Absolutely amazing. What a fantastic ship the Seabourn Legend was too. Expensive but, oh, it was fabulous. George was in seventh heaven, what an amazing start to that holiday. Like George's love of fast and expensive cars, I used to say to him that we had worked hard and earned our money. His life expectancy was dubious, so I reckoned that if that's how he wanted to spend it, on cars and luxury travel, it was our decision to do as we liked.

Another spell was spent at Harefield in the autumn when George was quite poorly, this time a leaky heart valve was diagnosed, but not sufficiently serious to require surgery, merely a rebalancing of pill regime. However, a worrying incident happened whist he was there. Our solicitor rang to say that completion of the sale of the land to the rear of The Key House was imminent and he wanted the bank account details to pay the money in. I thought it a bit strange as he knew our bank details so I said to just go ahead and put the money into our joint account, and we would sort out where to invest the money later. He told me that George had opened a separate account in his sole name, and he wanted the money to go in there. I objected and said no, this was a jointly owned piece of land and that the money had to go into our account in order to use our annual Capital Gain Allowance. He contradicted me saying that when we originally purchased the Key House in 2008, George had put the house and garden area into our joint names but had separated the orchard area and had that contract put into his name only. I was furious, saying that this was not right, how had that happened without my knowledge, particularly as we had bought The Key House with a bridging loan in our joint names, but I now find out that it wasn't what I had understood. I would never have agreed to have put myself into a vulnerable financial position if I had known what George was doing. Why had he done that? The money from the sale of the land was designated to pay for the renovation of the jointly owned home, so why put the money into a separate sole account? It did not make any sense. But as I soon realised, there were a lot of things that George had done recently that did not make any sense. And much worse was yet to come.

George was discharged from hospital, genuinely concerned obviously about this leaky heart valve, but we came home, and life carried on much as before. I said little more about the money in his bank as it never occurred to me that there was anything sinister.

Hm, I should have heard big warning bells. I should have investigated what was going on, should have trusted myself to look after my affairs

But I didn't.

2011

February saw us on holiday again in Tenerife. After xmas every year George decided he had had enough of English winter, the cold damp and dark. In years past we would go off on a skiing holiday. It was a sport we both loved and had lots of fun with friends on the slopes but as Georges' health became more compromised, he favoured finding warmth and sun. The builders could not work because of the cold and George felt the benefit of the sunshine so off we went for a week. It is not my favourite place in the world, but I know it has good medical facilities and the shortest flight to get somewhere warm. Uneventful but nice to see the sun.

Work started on the orchard wall when we returned, I called it the Great Wall of China. It was the boundary between the garden and the orchard that we had sold for housing development. As we had beautiful old stone walls on either side of the house running the length of the garden, it was the most appropriate thing to do to continue the stone wall across the boundary. It was a massive undertaking, tons and tons of stone had to be bought and our stonemason, a lovely guy, who was an absolute artist in stone walling, did a fantastic job. He was a bit of a law unto himself. When he was at work he was meticulous, a brilliant stonemason, however when paid at the end of the week, he would go straight to the pub, spend his earnings there till it had all gone and then he'd just turn up when he sobered up, as if nothing had happened, so really it was about every other week that he was working. Subsequently the wall took what seemed for ever to build but it was an amazing job. I got terribly upset with the developers as there was a magnificent weeping willow tree and a huge eucalyptus tree on the land that we had sold. They insisted that we removed them before the deal could be done and so one day, I returned from the weeks food shopping to find these beautiful trees cut down. I was devastated, how sad that those exquisite trees had to be sacrificed, together with all the lovely old apple and pear trees in the orchard, for a row of soulless, new build houses. But it put a lot of money in the bank – George's bank!!!

Our builders had also started the construction of the new garage, again a huge job, built on the site of the original dovecote and took for ever for the planning and conservation permissions to be granted. As this was being built, at the same time, George had ideas and plans for the old garage, which had become a workshop and lean - too greenhouse over the years. So, as plans and ideas developed, we agreed that we needed to put in an electricity supply at the same time as the new garage. That entailed digging a trench across the driveway from the new garage to the old one. That meant that the drive looked even more of a mess than before. The original drive was a mish mosh of concrete, earth, compounded gravel and bits of old tarmac patching up. George decided that he wanted a new and smart drive, which I totally agreed with. We always had lovely cars, it added value to the house and aesthetically enhanced the look of the property. I would have liked a gravel drive but, as it was all on a slope, that was totally impractical. When it rained, all the gravel would have followed gravity and ended up on the road. The logical solution was a complete tarmac drive. Red tarmac would enhance the look of the black and white Tudor property but was at an extortion cost.

George had finally agreed to replace my old Renault as it kept breaking down. George exchanged a Jaguar for an Aston Martin then a Bentley, back to a Jaguar then another Bentley. I never minded as George's love was for his cars and his health had been so compromised, it was his main joy. I always got to drive the fabulous cars, but my car was a little Renault convertible, which was great fun, but it was becoming a liability. He went off to the auctions one day and rang me to say he had bought me a Mercedes. I was thrilled. It was a CLS, beautiful lines, a very elegant limousine. It was fabulous to drive, and I was a very happy bunny until...

I had a doctor's appointment; it was still February and we were going through a particularly cold snap. I went off to the village in sleety weather and parked at the bottom of the surgery car park for my 4pm appointment. Some 45 minutes later I came out to find heavy snow falling. I got into this beautiful car, started the engine but it would not grip on the ice, just wheels spinning round, and I could not get up the slope. I got out, walked to the local Co Op to buy salt; they were out of stock. So I bought 2 bags of dishwasher salt (how much??), walked, or rather slid, back down the slope to the car, sprinkling the salt from each hand, trying to judge the trajectory and width of the car so the wheels could grip. I got back in the car and waited a few minutes till I saw the salt doing its job and 2 melted tracks appeared. The car drove beautifully up the slope and I got home. However, the drive off the road up to the house was even steeper than the car park. I had to abandon the car, half on the road, half on the pavement, struggle up to the house, get the dogs towels and old blankets to lay on the drive so that the car could grip and, with much wheel spinning, swerving, cursing and swearing, I got the car up the drive. This all took well over an hour. I finally walked into the house, cold and bad tempered, to be greeted with "where the hell have you been, I haven't had a cup of tea all afternoon". I blew my top, I was grumpy, wet and very cross. Not often know for outbursts of anger, I am very even tempered normally but … When I gathered myself, I said, "sorry George, that car has to go. It is beautiful to look at and drive – in good weather. In snow, ice and steep driveways, it is bloody useless. From now on you can drive it, I'm driving the Bentley which is 4-wheel drive". As a thought, though not voiced I said to myself "and what was wrong with putting the kettle on yourself? I'm not your servant and you are perfectly capable". George amazingly agreed with me and we started the research to buy me another car. I think it was the idea of him relinquishing his Bentley to me that swung it! It was at this time that the new Range Rover Evoque was being launched so we went off to have a look and agreed it would be perfect. So, I put my name down but had to wait several months for it to be built. I really was a happy bunny this time and so excited at the prospect of having my new car.

April saw spring arrive, and George was very keen to go to Monaco again, we loved the French Riviera and so I rented the usual apartment in Villefranche and off we went, driving the Bentley over, with Bennion, our Jack Russell, had lots of fun as usual for the whole month of May, going to the Monaco Grand Prix, the bi-annual Historic race weekend, seeing lots of likeminded racing friends, the sunshine and the sea.

I had always been keen to buy a small place in the South of France, but property was monumentally expensive. This time George was in total agreement. He said we could use some of the money from the sale of Lowes House if we could find somewhere within our budget. We looked at lots of property whilst we were there and found a ground floor flat under construction. It was part of a lovely old house that was being renovated and turned into 3 apartments. It was perfect. Three beds, lovely kitchen, 2 bathrooms, living room opening onto a small garden with a pool and fantastic sea views, and in Villefranche which is where we loved to be. We offered the asking price, arranged to see a lawyer, but then the developer decided to pull out of the deal. The estate agent was absolutely furious, said it was illegal as the law in France stated that if we had offered the asking price, then it became an automatic contract so did we want to sue the developer for breach of contract. We said no, what was the point of spending loads of money on a French lawyer to sue an Italian developer, from UK? That would just be madness and throwing money away. So, we nearly bought a flat in France but not quite. If we had gone through with the purchase and tied up a lot of our savings, life for me could have been vastly different now.

We had a fabulous time at the British GP in July and in August had a great day in Edinburgh, being flown there by a friend's private jet, went all around the Royal Yacht and had a fantastic lunch at The Witchery, a very well-known and renowned restaurant. All in all, we had a dreadfully expensive but fabulous year. George was, quite rightly, aware that his life span was very uncertain, so felt entitled to spend our hard earned money on doing what he wanted, fortunately he was quite well for most of the time thank goodness, so he was able to enjoy himself. Me too!

There is a purpose to most of the ramblings in this chapter which will be realised as the story unfolds.

Just to summarise that in 2010/11 we spent an enormous amount of money: -

New drive £10,000

The Great Wall of China £10,000

Bentley number 1 £120,000

Jaguar £25,000

Aston Martin £40,000

Bentley number 2 £80,000

Mercedes £20,000

Range Rover Evoque £30,000

Seaborn Cruise £12,000

Other asstd holidays - approx. £10,000

= £352,500

Sales of cars amounted to around £140,000

So, give or take, we spent around £200,000 - money which I was later accused of stealing and that I had to account for in court!!!

Sadly, George's health started to deteriorate again in the autumn and at his annual check-up at Harefield Hospital in November, the doctor was quite concerned by the leaky heart valve so decided that after Christmas they would have him in to have further tests to see if anything could be done.

2012

George was admitted in early February, initially for a week of tests. I booked a room at the hostel and the regime of hospital life once more became the norm. The doctors had conferences about him, ran tests, scratched their heads about how to resolve the issue. Leaking heart valves are quite common and under normal circumstances, a relatively easy remedy with surgery to repair the leak. George, of course, was the exception. I am a layman here so only relaying what the doctors told me in so called easy to understand terminology. George had been given a heterotopic heart transplant. This, more commonly known as a piggyback transplant, meant that Georges' original heart was left in intact and a second heart was inserted into the chest cavity and "plumbed" in so that the 2 hearts worked in tandem. The leaking valve was in his original heart, but the doctors could not get to it to repair it due to all the interconnective "plumbing" between the two hearts.

I hope you can follow what I am trying to explain here. The doctors were more concerned about damaging the interconnecting vessels by trying to surgically repair the faulty valve. George was, as I have previously said, becoming increasingly mentally fragile, determined to stay in hospital, refusing to leave, until he was mended. We were sent home a couple of times, only for George to insist I took him back in. Each time it was a 2-hour drive. I think, on reflection, that he was very scared that if he did not get the surgery to mend the valve he was going to die. He was quite delusional at times, absolutely determined that the doctors could fix this problem. "Find a way "he used to say. He would not accept that there was nothing they could do. This went on for months and we were there until almost the end of July. I came back and forth to deal with builders, mail, laundry, see my kids, my mother and father, so I wore a path up and down the MI and M25 again. Eventually the doctors agreed to try surgery and George was delighted. This was the week after the British Grand Prix so, about the second week of July. He had his pre op, everything was set for Thursday morning but when the anaesthetist arrived that morning and looked at all the test results from the day before, he concluded that George's kidney function was so poor that he would not survive the anaesthetic. So, it was cancelled at the 11th hour. George went into orbit. He was beyond devastated, he was irrational, told the staff they were trying to kill him because he said without that surgery he would die. He shouted, ranted and raved. They called in the medical councillor to try to talk to him and explained that he could go home and live out the rest of his life, and if he was careful, could possibly have another 5 years or so. Then they discharged him back to the care of the GP back at home. His parting vitriolic words to the staff was "you are sending me home to die". I had to try and talk to him to say that they had done a fantastic job for him, cared for him over all the years of his transplant but that they are humans, not miracle workers. He should live his life, enjoy every day, we none of us know how long we have got on this planet.

George was not having any of it. He was completely unbalanced, unhinged, incapable of thinking about anything or anyone else. I suggested that as we had been incarcerated from February till July in hospital, we had missed spring at home and early summer. I suggested that we should get on a cruise ship from Southampton, easy, as we just drove there with no airports to negotiate. A porter greeted you at the entrance to the port and took away your luggage, the car was valet parked and you just collected your ships pass and found your way to your cabin, usually having been greeted as you embarked with a glass of champagne. Wonderful. It was just escape from the incarceration of the past months, for a couple of weeks. That appealed, as a holiday always did for George, and so we got a last-minute deal on P and O Azura. A bit of a mistake in hindsight. It was the middle of August, over 3000 passengers and half of them were school kids on their holidays. Peace and quiet it was not. The pool was always jam packed, the noise was at ear splitting decibel level, the buffet was always crammed and the night club too but we managed to find quiet spots, the weather was lovely, George rested in bed most afternoons and so I could swim, read or mooch around the shops at the various ports of call. A much-needed break after 7 months of hospital life as you become institutionalised.

When we got home, we had to go and register with the palliative care consultant. She gave us both a lot of advice and help to face the future. George was not going to get any better than he already was and we both knew that he would gradually deteriorate. His brain was definitely not working properly, he was not capable of driving any more. He would get in the car, get to the bottom of the drive and say, "do I turn left or right?" I would say "well where are you going?" He knew where he wanted to go but had no idea how to get there. He was unbelievably bad tempered, exceedingly difficult to please, in fact, exceedingly difficult to live with.

I talked to all 4 of our kids and called for a family meeting. Ann said that I was just making a fuss; there was nothing wrong with her dad. That was an absolute denial of the situation till I explained, without pulling any punches, that George was indeed deteriorating, he was terminally ill, was under the care of the Palliative Care Consultant and I needed her to play her part in the ongoing care of her father. I needed help. As simple as that. George's brother, Chris, who lived about an hour north of us, asked if he could come and help by taking George out or just by visiting and I, naively, thought, how kind. So gradually Ann, John and Chris became much closer to George after that and I was so pleased, thinking that they were all being caring and helping me out. My kids, David and Alison were also willing to help whenever needed. Alison had announced a couple of months previously that she and her partner, were going to have a baby. I was going to be a grandma!!! Wow, I was ecstatic, what wonderful news amongst all the difficulties, doom and gloom. A beacon of light and hope for the future.

I was very absorbed and busy with preparations for a Women's Motor Racing Club Ball to celebrate 50 years of the Doghouse Club. This took a great deal of time and effort but thoroughly enjoyable and a complete distraction for me as Chairman and something to take my mind off Georges health. This was held in October, at Silverstone. A black-tie event, wonderfully supported, with amazing sponsorship, and the night was a huge success. We raised £20,000 for the nominated charities for the year. Wow. George enjoyed the evening in the company of many of his racing friends but when I look back at the photos of the event I realise how poorly, and thin George looked that night.

Ann, John and Chris continued to visit often, although my relationship with Ann was not so good, nothing new there. She asked, what I regarded, very impertinent questions about our finances, which I firmly told her was our business and not hers. She wanted to know how much we were spending on the house, the holidays, the cars and my personal things, like clothes and shoes. Chris was always concerned about our finances and investments as well which I found very disturbing. I said to him on one occasion, "Chris I don't ask you about your pension and savings, why are you so keen to know about ours, I find it very intrusive that you are getting so involved?" He replied to the effect that he had been a financial advisor so knew what he was talking about. In fact, he had been an insurance salesman, had 2 businesses in the past both of which had failed, so not a lot of experience or expertise for us to follow. George just said he was trying to help.

I should have smelt a rat then, but I didn't, I just thought they were being impertinent.

November was grim, damp, early snow, dark nights and George wanted to go somewhere warm. "Get us on a ship out of here and fast" he said. The Queen Mary was sailing from Southampton on a three-week cruise to Madeira and Tenerife. So, I booked us on and off we went. Chris was very disapproving of me saying that I was always finding ways of spending George's money and of being a spendthrift. I basically told him to butt out, it was our money, George had wanted to go away, it was his idea and what on earth was it to do with him. Away from the cold and the family

George was as happy as Larry. He loved cruising, the food, lots of new people to meet and talk to. He could retell times of when he was a racing driver and his health issues. People were always interested in his heart transplant tales. They were, and still are, amazing stories.

We got home in early December and of course it was full on to get Xmas together. I had asked if all the kids could be with us this year as I knew that it just might be / could be, George's last one. Everyone agreed and I made a supreme effort to make it as supersonic as possible. There were no stops that I did not pull out.

Presents were fabulous, food wonderful, xmas tree amazing. Everything was perfect. Alison was by this time getting quite large, we knew she was having a little boy, Oscar, and he was due at the end of March. It was lovely to get the whole family together and although George got tired very quickly, he enjoyed having everyone there, including John's new girlfriend, Jane. The only person that seemed to be uncomfortable was John. He did not join in the conversation much, could not look any of us in the eye. He was definitely not ok. I didn't know why, didn't ask and it just went out of my head. I was too busy trying to keep xmas day running smoothly. I just thought it all a bit odd. "Perhaps he's had a spat with Jane" I mused, and then never gave it another thought till some months later.

So, Xmas came and went, and so did the end of the year.

2013 ANNUS HORRIBILUS

There are no words to describe this year adequately. Adjectives like horrendous, devastating, dreadful, terrible, they do not even come close. As I write this in 2020, I am still traumatized, and think I always will be. Over it, yes, moved on, yes, but there are still nights when I wake up shaking and in tears. How did it happen, how could it happen, how could I have been so stupid? Eye off the ball. I do not know to this day, but it did.

Winter

January 2nd, blissfully unaware of what was going on behind my back, I decided that as 2014 was going to be our Silver Wedding Anniversary Year I needed a plan to aim for. Wow, what an achievement that would be, with both of us having second marriages and considering George's health issues, it was a miracle and although George's brain was deteriorating, his body was stable. No further heart issues, a couple of mini strokes in the year before but nothing dramatic. So, I started researching for the perfect trip. In the Sunday Times I found it. Train from East Midlands Parkway Station to St Pancras. Chauffeur driven car to the London Ritz for afternoon tea, a theatre show, late supper and overnight at the Ritz. Chauffeur driven car back to St. Pancras, Eurostar to Paris 1st Class, Orient Express to Venice, 3 nights in the Cipriani Hotel in Venice and then 7 nights Seabourn cruise around the Croatian coast, business class flight back and chauffeur driven car home. Fabulous!

At £5,000 each it was a bit of a gulp, but I thought "why not". It would be a huge milestone. So, I booked it and paid the deposit. Keep this as a big surprise for 2014, I thought.

January 4th Having done all the research for the proposed Silver Wedding treat I was feeling pleased with myself. We had had a good Xmas with all the family, lots of socialising over the New Year and the plans in place for the following years anniversary. I went off to the hairdressers on the Friday afternoon. It was my regular appointment at 2pm for a hairdo followed by a cup of tea and a cream cake from "Birds" with mum and dad afterwards. George always used to say every week "oh it must be bloody Friday; I expect you're going to see your mother then! To which I always used to reply, "I only see mum and dad for 1 hour a week, I have 45 minutes at the hairdressers to get out of the house, catch up on all the village gossip and get my hair done. It's cheaper than therapy and I always bring you a blackcurrant cream cake home !!!"

Usually I was late, rushing around to get everything done before I left home but on this particular day, I had picked up the post from the letter box on the gate, and was parked outside the hairdressers 10 minutes early so decided to open the mail. A couple of things for George, the usual junk mail headed straight for the bin and a letter addressed to me. I opened it to find a letter from our solicitor. Not addressed to us both as would be usual but just to me. Intrigued I read on.

Back track to a couple of weeks before Christmas. Chris, George's brother, had visited and George told me that Chris was driving him to see our solicitor as he was trying to "put his house in order". At the time I had said that I thought I ought to have taken him, this was our business, but Chris said no, I was too busy with Christmas preparations, so, although a bit miffed, I thought nothing more about it. That evening, in conversation George said that he had been to see the solicitor, had tweaked his will and that he would be confirming all to me in the New Year. So, when I opened the letter it was not unexpected and as I have already said I was intrigued to know what George had done.

When George and I got married in 1989, we had made identical wills, If I died first then all would go to George in his lifetime and then following his death, all that was left would be divided equally between the 4 kids and Georges' will said exactly the same; all would come to me then be divided 4 ways when I went. Absolutely fair and reasonable, particularly relevant now after 24 years of marriage..

I said the letter was not unexpected and I was intrigued; I was not prepared, however, for the bombshell though. George had not only changed his will completely, cutting me out completely; he had changed the ownership of our properties too. All the houses we had bought and sold over the years; we had always put the development properties in the company name but always had our main house in our joint names. We were married; why wouldn't we? George, advised by Chris, had changed the ownership of our jointly owned home and another rental property, from joint names to tenants in common.

He had also cut out any legacy to my children David and Alison.

If you own a house jointly, on the death of one party the property ownership automatically reverts to the other party. If you are married there is no inheritance tax applicable. If you own a property as tenants in common, then you can arrange to leave your half to whoever you like. George had willed his half to his 2 children Ann and John and not to me.

I was baffled and didn't understand how this could be done without my knowledge or permission, so I phoned the solicitor to ask what was going on. I was, understandably, not only worried, I wanted to know how this had happened and what the implications were. I was assured that this was perfectly legal but that he thought that George had already discussed this with me.

No, he had not.

So, I asked, bearing in mind George's prognosis, realistically what this meant, if and when George died.

"Oh, its ok, you can stay in the house for as long as you live" I was assured. Great.

"What if I want to sell the house to buy something smaller, can I use any financial differential to buy another rental property to provide extra income?"

"No" was the answer. "If you sell, then half the proceeds automatically go to his children immediately "

"So, that means that I am condemned to live in a house that's too big and expensive to run, that I never wanted to live in the first place and all the money that I've earned in my lifetime with George has to be given to his family before I die?"

"Yes, I suppose so".

"So, if I was to die before George, in my will I've left him everything, so then when he dies, he doesn't have to leave my children anything?"

"Yes, that's right, you need to change your will immediately".

By the time the conversation had finished I was sitting in my car shaking with horror and rage. What the hell have you done, George, without discussing this and the implications with me. How could you have sat through Christmas and not told me what you have done. Where was your brain, how dare you? It was like a nightmare. I am not sure how I sat being pleasant to my lovely hairdresser, talking banalities, when my world was crashing in on me. How did I go to Mum and Dads and sit politely drinking tea? I have no idea. I can't remember; it has erased itself from my memory. I got in the car to drive home wondering how to broach the subject when I got home, I should not have worried. My brain and mouth just took over.

I walked in the door, blew my top and yelled at the top of my voice "George what the bloody hell have you done? You had better sort this mess out now. I want the houses back in joint names now. I want your will reverting to how it was. This is appalling. How the hell did you expect me to agree to all this, how dare you?" I ranted, shouted, screamed, cried, was totally hysterical. "Why? Why? Why? I have worked with you, loved you, cared for you through thick and thin. You haven't thought through the implications, how can I live under a cloud like this when you die?" I went on and on, completely distraught. I was trembling, shaking, I was scared at where George's brain was. All he could say was that he had taken advice from his brother. "What's any of this to do with Chris" I asked, "he's been bankrupt twice, never made a halfpenny in his life, "why are you listening to him and it's none of his business". I am your wife; things like this should be discussed and agreed with between us. We had always talked about everything, no secrets. We have always had a joint account, everything open and above board, not his - or hers, just ours."

There was no budging him. He was convinced that it was all done for my benefit and all absolutely legal. He could not see or understand what I was so upset about. I really began to believe that his brain was seriously impaired that he could be so misled. All the times in the past when he had despaired of Chris saying that his business brain was sadly lacking. I had always known that Chris was jealous of our success and begrudged our way of life. This was his revenge.

George rang Chris to say how angry and upset I was and over the next few days I had a barrage of unpleasant phone calls from Chris, accusing me of being greedy, wanting the money for myself, saying that I spent too much money on clothes, wasting money on frivolous holidays and basically poking his nose into our business. I was really angry and upset about all this because the holidays were always George's idea as he loved to travel and, yes, I had nice clothes, so did George; it was our hard earned money and up to us how it was used and I just didn't know where to turn. I discussed the situation with best friends, Robert and Lindsay who were aghast at the situation.

So, the atmosphere between George and I continued to be frosty. George was intransigent, could not see my point of view about Chris's interference and what had been done without my knowledge, discussion or permission. From then on, I became the enemy. George always had liked to think he made all the decisions and hated to be crossed. He always wanted to be right, would never back track or admit that maybe he was wrong.

Sunday 13th was a relatively quiet and peaceful day, with a nice lunch and the papers. George always read the car section and found a Bentley for sale at a dealership in Manchester. I was buzzing in and out of the kitchen cooking and I heard George on the phone. He was arranging to go and look at this car on the following day, Monday. I interrupted him saying that we could not go on the Monday because he had a consultant's appointment and I had my tri annual appointment at the Breast Cancer Screening unit. I said, make it for Tuesday and I will drive you, walked off back into the kitchen to carry on cooking. Over lunch I asked him why he wanted to go to Manchester to look at another Bentley when he had only recently bought an absolute beauty, just before Christmas. He just wanted to go and see it so it was agreed we would go on the Tuesday.

Jan 14th Monday morning came. For the first time in over 20 years of George being ill, it turned out that George's appointment locally clashed with mine. George said it was fine, he was happy to drive himself as it wasn't far, he knew where to go and so we were both in the process of leaving when George said he was just going to go and see the builders before he left. I told him not to forget his appointment letter and put it on the hall table, so off I went. I prompted Woody, our builder to not let George be late setting off.

I was on my way down the M1, about half an hour later when my phone rang. It was the Palliative Care Consultant. Did I know where George was? I explained that for the first time ever I was not accompanying George as I had my appointment and that he was supposed to be coming by himself and should have been there already. She had tried his mobile phone as well as the home line but got no answer. I suggested that I rang the builder to see if he had got waylaid, I know George, he used to lose all sense of time on the building site, so I put the phone down and rang Woody. He confirmed that George had left well over half an hour before and should be at the hospital by now. I rang the consultant back to say not to worry, he had probably got stuck in traffic. I had arrived at my appointment so said I would ring her back when I had finished. I was in and out within about 20 minutes, so rang her back fully expecting George to be there. He was not. My phone battery was almost drained, so I said I would get back home and ring her again.

When I pulled onto the drive of the Key House, I found a police car parked. You can imagine all the things flying through my mind, oh no, he's had a car accident, he shouldn't be driving, he's not capable Oh, I'm to blame, I should have gone with him and cancelled my appointment. I was fearing the worst.

I got out of the car, my heart pounding, and so did the police officer. I searched his face and he spoke first. "do you know where George is" he asked. "No" I said, "why are you here?" He explained that because George was classed as terminally ill, the consultant was legally obliged to inform the police if he did not turn up to an appointment and could not be contacted. We went indoors and he started to tell me what had transpired. As technically we live in Leicestershire, but he was attending a hospital in Derbyshire, but his route would have taken him through Nottinghamshire, all three counties police forces had been alerted. I had to give the registration number of the Bentley and they were out searching for him as a potential missing person. By this time, I was worried sick. George had his phone with him, but he had left the appointment letter on the hall table. I phoned John and asked him to keep trying his dads' number. He didn't seem unduly perturbed, obviously not appreciating the seriousness of the matter. I phoned Ann to tell her that her dad had gone missing and said how worried I was. I won't repeat her response, but it was not what I expected, she was just rude and pretty abusive. I thought she would be worried too but she thought I was making mountains out of mole hills, that I was stupid and causing a fuss. I was even accused of having reported him missing to the police. It absolutely was not me, but she did not believe me. Lindsay saw the police car on the drive and came over to see if she could help. We sat trying to work out where the dickens he had gone, then suddenly, about 2 hours later, I had a blinding flash of realisation. "I know where he is, he's in Manchester, gone to look at this car". I shot into the sitting room and picked up the car section of the Sunday Times to find the article torn out, which meant I didn't know which garage it was but fortunately Lindsay had a copy at home so ran to get it. We pieced together, like a jigsaw, the missing advert, which gave the name, address and phone number of the garage. I was going to ring but the police officer wouldn't let me. He said it was now a police enquiry and they would handle it. So, the police phoned and, sure enough, George was there, having just bought another Bentley. The policeman told the owner that George wasn't to leave until they got there. So, we had the Manchester police force involved as well!

The police escorted George to the police station. They spoke to his consultant who advised that, in his condition, without his medication (he had not taken his antirejection drugs that morning), he should not drive home. So, the police said they would either get him into hospital to provide him with the appropriate pills or get him to come home by taxi but would not allow him to drive. George was beside himself with fury but had to agree to get a taxi. The police officer stayed with me till he arrived home, the taxi cost over £200 and he had to leave both the cars in Manchester. He was appallingly rude to me, blaming me for reporting him missing. He, like Ann, would not believe that it was the doctor that had informed the police. Whilst George was coming home by taxi, I tried asking the garage owner if he would kindly reverse the car sale, telling him that George was very unwell and not quite mentally capable of handling his affairs, but he refused saying that he had seemed perfectly reasonable. However, under the circumstances, he arranged for both Bentleys to be returned to us on a low loader, free of charge. Great, I thought, how considerate. It was obvious through the police intervention that all was not well. It would not have taken much for him to have cancelled the transaction and refunded the bank draft.

So, we ended up with 2 Bentleys, George hopping mad and blaming me for interfering, oh life was going from bad to worse. Not a good start to the New Year. I was then absolutely convinced that George was suffering from the beginnings of Dementia. I asked the consultant if I could talk to her privately. Oh, patient confidentiality, I understand the reasoning behind it but when you are married and voicing concerns about your husband's behaviour, it is impossible to find any help and support. The consultant, however, came up trumps. She asked me to write down all my concerns and put it in a private letter to her. Whilst she couldn't report back to me, at least she could be aware of what I was worried about. I wrote chapter and verse about all the accusations, the verbal abuse, the car incident, the wills incident and lots of minor little niggles that added up to the big picture. She was concerned about George driving and instructed the GP to test George's cognisance. The GP visited and I was accused afterwards saying that I was trying to take his licence away. Unbeknown to me was that also someone in the village had reported to the doctors' surgery that George was seemingly unable to drive properly and had voiced concerns. George told the doctor, in no uncertain terms that he would drive regardless of what anybody said he should or shouldn't do.

I was pretty nearly at my wits end. I was being harangued by George on a daily basis, if not on a minute by minute basis; I really had become public enemy Number 1, I was mentally exhausted with trying to care for him and yet being insulted not only by him but by his daughter and brother as well. One afternoon, about 4 o'clock, I'd just made a cup of tea and given George a piece of cake, I sat down with a quilt I was embroidering for baby Oscar, minding my own business when George suddenly looked at me with a scarily, wild look on his face, picked up the phone and dialled Ann. When she answered he started crying down the phone, still looking me straight in the face, and said "Ann, you've got to come and help me, she's hurting me, she's hitting me and I'm black and blue". I sat there in total disbelief, grabbed the phone off him and told her that I was doing no such thing; I was sat with a cup of tea doing my sewing and he was eating a piece of cake. Ann is the other side of London, over 3 hours' drive away, and hasn't got a clue what is going on, but she obviously took her father's side and wondered what the hell I was up too. I have to put myself in her shoes to understand what she felt, unable to see for herself what was going on.

I had to get away for a few days or I would have cracked up. I needed some time out, fresh air and peace and quiet. I could not worry Alison with my troubles, she was 7 months pregnant, so I spoke to my brother, found a last-minute rental deal on a cottage in Yorkshire, near Whitby, on a farm. I packed the car, loaded the dog, picked up my brother and headed north. Oh, I will hasten to add that I prepared 7 dinners and 7 lunches and put them in the freezer with microwave instructions on each for George, I arranged a visitor every day and friends Lindsay, Robert and other close friends to come over every day to check up on him. His medication was all put out for him so he could manage on his own. I thought my brain would explode if I did not get away.

Henry, my brother, and I arrived at this charming little cottage; we had brought supplies from Marks and Spencer's, firewood for the log burner and we settled in. The following morning we were thigh deep in snow so not going anywhere. The peace was wonderful, the dog made friends with the farmers dog and we lost him in the snow, he couldn't jump high enough, so lots of laughter and I felt my shoulders slowly descending from either side of my ears. I was so tense and wound up. It is amazing the restorative effect that a few days away from the source of the problem, fresh air, fabulous views and peace. I could breathe. No shouting, blaming, accusing, just peace. John phoned me to see where I was. George had clearly phoned him to say that I had just left him in the lurch, I had abandoned him. I again had to tell him that all was taken care of, I would never abandon him; he was an extremely sick man. I just needed some time out. All lovely things must come to an end, and I drove home. George was thrilled to see me, greeted me as if nothing was wrong so, let sleeping dogs lie and quietly get on with life as best I could. The end of January came, and February passed relatively peacefully.

Towards the end of February George made a very startling and strange announcement. He wanted to give David and Alison £50,000 each out of our joint pension investment fund. I said that was a very lovely gesture, but it was illegal to give away that much money in one go, the legal gift allowance was about £8,000 per year and so I would have to investigate how it could be done. I also said I didn't want the money to come out of our pension fund as it would incur penalties to withdraw it before the investment term was over so why don't we take it out of the HSBC account that George had put the sale of the land money into. He said no. I asked him if he was giving Ann and John the same amount and he said he had already done it. I was very concerned about the legal ramifications as his life span was a bit precarious, not likely to survive for the 7 years required to not incur tax, and if he'd already taken the money from the HSBC account for them why didn't he want the money to David and Alison to come from the same source. There should have been well over £450,000 in that current account with no penalties for withdrawals. Also, why had he given away our money without discussing it with me first?

The last day of February saw George's sister come for a 2-day visit. After the first day, she could see what I was dealing with, but thought how kind it was of Chris, her brother, as well, to come and spend time with George. Not much I could say really, she didn't know the ins and outs of the legal and financial shenanigans that had gone off. I did not want to discuss it with her; it was not her business any more than it was Chris's. Anyway, she asked me to keep her posted and said she would come and see us again soon.

Sunday 3rd March was my lovely Dad's 90th birthday and we had planned a great meal out, all the family there other than George. He said he didn't feel up to it, but the reality was that he didn't want to see any of my family as he knew that they knew how dreadfully he was behaving towards me and that my father was very angry with what he'd done over the properties. Dad, a very wise owl, warned me to be suspicious of his motives but also said that I needed to get professional care for George as he was definitely showing signs of irrationality and I couldn't handle this on my own. I assured Dad that I had, on the quiet, been contacted by the Palliative Care Consultant, who had instructed a social worker to monitor George's behaviour and temper. George resented it but accepted that it wasn't me but the doctor who was concerned. He actually said to this lovely lady, hilariously, that he was genuinely worried about MY state of mind!!!!

She quietly gave me her contact number and agreed that I would keep a diary of events and phone her on a weekly basis so she could see what was going on. I had several private meetings with her and fortunately she witnessed a couple of Georges' irrational moments for herself.

March 14th I had made an appointment to see our solicitor as George had altered his will, so I needed to alter mine now that the properties were in a different legal ownership. Sadly, I had to cut George out of my will in order to leave my share of the money to my children. I talked to him about the money that George had given his children and he confirmed that it wasn't legal to do that and that he would speak to George. I also asked him why it was legal for one party to change the legal joint ownership of a property without the other party's knowledge. He said it was perfectly legal, but that George had assured him that I was in agreement, and that it had been discussed beforehand. He was most upset that I didn't know till after the event and agreed that George was behaving badly. I said, irrational, and that I suspected, although it had not been formally diagnosed with, the onset of Dementia. The lawyer, who was a personal friend, as well as our legal advisor said that if he had been diagnosed previously, then he could not have taken legal instructions from him. He did say that his brother, Chris did most of the talking at the time, and that George had just agreed with him. I warned him to be careful about any other instructions George might undertake in the future and please would he get in touch with me if that happened. I obviously put him into an exceedingly difficult position, and he felt that, sadly, he would be unable to act for either of us in the future. So, my will did not get changed and I knew I'd have to find someone else to act for me. I was sad as we had had a lovely relationship with him in the past, but I did understand his situation.

I wasn't too worried at that point in time, I was much more focused on the arrival of my Grandson, Oscar. He was due around the 22nd March. My first grandchild, so exciting and the thought took away all the stress and strain of what I was going through at home. A baby, a new life, oh how wonderful.

Spring

Monday 25th March I need to take a very deep breath before writing this next bit.

I had, a few weeks previously, had to have some minor hand surgery and on the 25th had to go to the hand clinic to have the plaster cast removed and have some physiotherapy. On my way to the hospital, Alison phoned me to say that she was on her way to the maternity unit. OOOOH I exclaimed "are things moving"? Alison said she didn't know but would keep me posted. My appointment was at 10 am and I was desperate to get it over with quickly. The cast was removed but I couldn't wait any longer to be seen and refused any physio saying I would do all the exercises myself; I was busting a gut to get out. It was after 11 am when I left and immediately rang Alison, no reply. I rang again, no reply. I rang and rang and rang. No reply. By 1 pm I was beside myself and had a terrible sense of foreboding. I should have learned by then that my instincts are always good. I somehow know when I don't need to worry and when I do. I had a blinding message in my head. Oscar has died. No, no, no, stop thinking like that, Alison is in labour and they haven't got time to answer the phone.

But I just knew.

Alison's partner Carl rang at 2 pm, absolutely distraught and sobbing down the phone. "can you come to the hospital now please, Oscar has died". I was in the car before I knew it, I phoned John and said I was on my way to the hospital, would he go and look after George, then I rang David, who was driving. I told him I needed to talk to him, please would he pull over and be parked safely. Then I told him. David and Alison are amazingly close. Closer than I have ever known a brother and sister. He was hysterical because he thought I had said that Alison had died. "No. No, it's Oscar" "Can you get to the hospital and meet me there. He just said that he was already on the way. I arrived about half an hour later, David was there in the waiting room, and Carl's father Gordon arrived a couple of minutes later. We were all in pieces, I am trembling as I write this, tears streaming down my face, just remembering. Carl eventually came into the waiting room to collapse with us all. He looked dreadful and then told us what had happened. I had imagined that Alison had gone into labour and that Oscar had died during childbirth. Even now, in the 21st century, giving birth can still be a dangerous and critical time. But that was not what had happened. Alison had gone to bed on Sunday but had not felt Oscar move all evening. Nor had he moved on Monday morning when she woke. Alison has also got an amazing 6th sense and was concerned enough to get herself to the hospital. She had not gone into labour at all. The nurse had felt no heartbeat when Alison got to the hospital and immediately called the doctor on duty and the consultant. Poor little soul had died; on the day he was due to be born. Oh, worse was then to come, if that was possible. Alison asked me to go into the room to see her. We both sat and sobbed. She was, understandably inconsolable. For 9 months she'd carried him, loved him, talked to him, played music to him. She had done the absolute best for him; she was a model mother. Her grief was terrible to see. Mine too; my little grandson who I would never know. We would never see him grow up. Eventually when she had calmed a little, we all sat with her. David was devastated too but relieved that Alison was ok, distraught but ok. The consultant came to see us to discuss what was to happen next. I honestly thought they would take Alison to theatre and perform a Caesarean Section, but no. They gave her some tablets to take and told us all to go home. The tablets would induce labour within 48 hours. I was aghast, how and why? She was going to have to go through all the pain and trauma of childbirth, knowing her precious little son was already dead. However much I try to rationalise this, I cannot. I thought it then, and still do, inhuman to put her through this. It is enough to mentally unhinge you. I am sure the maternity professionals have their reasons, but it seemed appalling, so uncaring, so cold, so unbelievable. Where was the tender understanding, nurturing, caring of someone who had just gone through the worst moment in life knowing she would have to then give birth a day or 2 later? So I took Carl and Alison home, Gordon took Carl's car back where we all sat for some time, all in a state of shock, at Alison and Carl's house, before she said she just wanted to put her head under the bedclothes. I told Carl to ring me, day or night as soon as the pills started to work.

I went home, still in shock, to tell George and John. John, as he and Alison were also remarkably close, was also terribly upset. We both cried. George was just quite cross that I hadn't cooked him any dinner! This was one of the occasions when you knew he was suffering from Dementia. He simply did not comprehend the situation. He said that women have miscarriages all the time, it wasn't anything special. However, I tried to explain that this was not a miscarriage, he just didn't get it. I said that Oscar was a full-term baby who had died, not just a few weeks of pregnancy. But I was talking out of my backside as usual. I said that I was going back to Alison's the following day and would stay with her as long as I was needed. So, of course, a row ensued that I was neglecting him. Talk about conflict. I arranged a friend to come over and sit with George. Where was my husband when I needed comfort and love? I was torn apart with grief. I had nursed George for over 23 years, cared, consoled, loved, but on the rare occasion that I needed support, understanding and love, there was none. I just wanted to be held, a shoulder to cry on, be comforted. But I knew then how sick his mind was but at that moment in time I was needed by my daughter.

26th March I went over to see Mum and Dad to tell them. Oh, more pain, they were so distraught too. Of course, they had been so looking forward to welcoming their first great grandson. I got my brother over to spend the rest of the day with them and then I drove up to Alison and Carl's house to find Alison in the early stages of labour. So off we went back to the hospital. I drove as Carl was in no fit state. We were ushered straight into the delivery suite. I stayed with them both until the last few minutes before Oscar arrived. It was their private time and I would have been an intrusion. I have never seen anyone go through labour like it. She had no pain relief; she hummed and breathed all the way through.

She never uttered a cry, not a shout, no hysterics, just a calm, focused way of getting herself through the worst imaginable situation anyone could imagine. I had the unenviable task of dealing with my ex-husband, Alison's father. He lived in Spain with his second wife and son but had booked a flight on the 26th to be in UK when his grandson was due to arrive. He had kept on phoning Alison's mobile and left umpteen messages, all of which had been ignored whilst Alison was going through labour. The atmosphere in that room was solemn, quiet, almost religious, although what little faith I had was destroyed during the past 36 hours. When Oscar was about to arrive, I left the room and phoned David to tell him the sad news. He of course was absolutely dumbstruck and terribly upset. I told him to go home (he still had a house in the UK), and I would phone him and keep him posted. He wanted to come straight to the hospital, but I insisted he didn't until Alison was ready to see him. That, of course, was very contentious, but I couldn't handle any of his histrionics; I'd had enough of that when I was married to him and certainly my emotions were already spread too thin to deal with anymore.

Eventually Carl came out and told me to go in. He was very emotional. "go and meet your grandson" he said. David had arrived after work along with Gordon and his wife. Carl said that he needed a beer and they all walked across the road to the pub for a break. I went in to see Alison sitting cross legged on the bed with little Oscar in her arms. As long as I live, I never want to see grief like that on my daughters' face: She was in mortal agony. Oscar was a perfect 7lb baby. He just looked like he was peacefully sleeping. Perfect in every way - except he wasn't breathing. I did not know how to bear it but needed to be strong for Alison. I could not break down. I just held him in my arms, put my arms around Alison and we cried quietly. All hers and my dreams slowly evaporating away. The little, so loved, boy who would never see his mummy or daddy, never see the sun and the rain, the day or night. I called him our little Peter Pan. David visited, Gordon and Catherine after, and then we left to give Alison and Carl private time with Oscar. Alison's father and his second wife briefly visited that evening after we had all left. Alison bathed Oscar and dressed him. He was allowed to stay in the room with them overnight but obviously had to be taken away the following morning. I went in at 9 am to take Alison and Carl home. The hardest thing in the world was for them to leave their baby there. I drove them home and made a cup of tea. Alison said, "go home Mum, you look exhausted too" and I was. She said she needed to go and get in the bath and talk to her body. It had carried and nurtured Oscar for 9 months and wanted to do the things a normal woman's body does after giving birth. In her usual, spiritual way, she lit candles and simply talked to her body to tell it what had happened.

We all deal with grief in our own way There is no right or wrong way. I was mentally, as well as physically, exhausted, having to be the strong one as usual, to keep Mum, Dad, Henry informed as well as friends. No caring words from George, just "what's for dinner"?

Keep it together. Breathe.

I had Alison's father on the phone, pontificating about where Oscar should be buried," that is their business" I told him but no, as usual, he wanted to interfere. I suppose that's an unkind thing to say as he was grieving too but he was a control freak and always wanted to take over and do things his way.

Keep it together. Breathe

I told him just to leave them alone for a few days.

Just leave me alone to grieve on my own too. Breathe.

The practicalities of course must be dealt with and everyone else's life carries on despite your life grinding to a halt.

Alison and Carl spent 27th and 28th just hiding in their own home but Carl knew he had to go to the registry office to register the birth and the death before any funeral arrangements could be made. Logically you must register a birth, obviously before a death. In Oscar's case though, he had died the day before he was born. Anyway, Carl phoned for an appointment only to be told that the following day was Good Friday and that the office would not be open again until the Easter Tuesday, which was a week after Oscar had died and that meant that no funeral plans could be put in place. Easter was a bit of a write off as you can imagine, George was grumpy and cross all the time because I was preoccupied, sad, just out of sorts. The last thing I felt like doing was a family Easter Sunday, so I didn't. I went to my brother who took the job over and had me, mum and Dad for lunch. George would not go.

Alison and Carl started the job of sorting out the funeral. The death certificate produced on 2nd April meant that all their plans could go ahead. The date for the funeral was Monday April 13th.

Alison's father played a blinder. His flight back to Spain was supposed to be on that date. He decided that Alison had planned the funeral deliberately to prevent him going. He couldn't possibly change his flight, could he? How much is a flight from East Midlands Airport to Malaga? Pennies in the great scheme of things but he chose to fly home and so he didn't attend. The funeral was devastating. Tiny little white wicker cradle / coffin buried in a consecrated woodland burial site near their home, a tree planted, and a poem read. The saving grace was that it was a lovely sunny spring morning with snowdrops in the woods and bulbs coming into bloom. We went back to Alison's, had a cup of tea and then went home, I took mum, dad and my brother back. George did not go to the funeral.

I went back home and George's words to greet me still ring in my ears. "I've seen enough of your miserable face over the past few weeks. I am sick of it, you have been no good to me, you'd better buck up your ideas".

Alison has not spoken to her father since before the funeral and who knows if she ever will. Just when she needed the most support in her life, he was not there for her.

<u>Late Spring</u>

I tried very hard not to have a miserable face, I tried very hard to make amends for my lack of care of George (it was all nonsense as everything had been arranged and organised for him, company, meals etc, I just hadn't been at his beck and call for a few weeks). I look back now and wonder how I did not completely crack up. But it was spring, I had lots to do in the garden to occupy my mind, and life pottered along.

George was apoplectic with rage a week after Oscars' funeral when we had a visit from a lovely lady called Julie.

She had been appointed by the Palliative Care consultant as Georges' care worker. He was genuinely nice to her and seemed to get on very well, so I was hugely relieved. Till she left, then, Oh, he went ballistic. "You got her involved, didn't you, you're trying to put me away, you're conspiring to get me put into a home, you're evil, I hate you". Oh, a barrage of insults. He phoned Ann to tell her I was trying to take his driving licence away; I was the root cause of all his problems, I really was the devil incarnate. So, I had both Ann and Chris, giving me chapter and verse about how I was treating George. Chris lives in Yorkshire and Ann in Surrey. They did not see George's irrational behaviour, his mood swings, they only knew what he was saying to them. Never once did either of them say to me "what can we do to help you". It was like a nest of vipers around me, almost a circling of vultures. I had nowhere to turn. I have friends who were incredibly supportive, God Bless Robert, Lindsay, Colleen and my family and particularly my 3 special Doghouse friends, Peta, Kate and Diane but still nobody really knows what goes on behind closed doors.

May 9th I thought it might be my last day. The Social Care Worker was overly concerned about George's deteriorating health, the leaking heart valve made George very tired and he spent more and more time in bed, so she instructed a Macmillan Nurse be assigned to George. She arrived to see George and he went skywards. This time I thought he was going to be physically violent: His temper was appalling, his language towards me was foul but he had never physically threatened me till then. That really frightened me. I did not know what George might be capable of. Tired and sick he may have been, but he was bigger and stronger than me.

When a temper is uncontrolled, it is amazing how violent you can be.

I just despaired and thought to myself, when is this nightmare ever going to end? I need some peace in my life, I am going to crack up, I cannot cope anymore. I am not getting any help from his family; quite the reverse, they were hateful towards me.

I talked to Mum, Dad and my brother who decided that I, and we all, needed to get away. We were all still grieving for Oscar and I was about to have a total breakdown. Dad suggested a cruise, so we found one going to The Norwegian Fjords. I thought, sea, mountains, calm, friendly company was just ideal. Fortunately, as it was likely to be cold in Norway, George had no interest in coming with us, just accused me of deserting my duty to him! Colleen and her sister said they would love to come too. I booked it, arranged for a care company to look after George, cooked and froze 7 days' worth of meals, put the dog in kennels as George would not look after him and would leave the gate open then I packed my suitcase and went.

I was due to do George's tax return and had got it almost totally up to date online before I went. I was just short of the bank statements for the HSBC account to get it complete. I said to George that he had to give me those statements or I could not file the tax return. I said if you get them for when I get back, I have just got a few days before the deadline. He said nothing….

I was so incredibly organized. How, I wonder with my brain in meltdown? The day we were due home was Sunday May 26th, Monaco Grand Prix day. I arranged for a Waitrose order to be delivered at 12 noon with a complete buffet lunch, champagne in the fridge, invited Robert and Lindsay and another friend, the race start was 1pm. Phew I hope I don't get delayed on the motorway on the way home, but knew that Lindsay would organise everything if I got held up.

So, the dog was in kennels, the race event was arranged, my suitcase packed and off we went. What a lovely week we had. Mum and Dad had not had a proper holiday for some years, not since the year that George had his stroke, neither had Henry. Colleen had not been away on holiday for, can you believe it, 30 years, and I was so in need of that break. We sat in fluffy white towelling dressing gowns on the cabin balcony with morning tea watching the amazing waterfalls coming off the mountain sides as we cruised in glorious sunshine along the fjords. It was soul restoring, calm, fun friends, family, laughter. No shouting, insults, demands, accusations, just blissful peace.

I arrived home with the Waitrose delivery man following me up the drive. Impeccable timing. George was thrilled to see me, loved the sweater that I had bought him, friends' round, lovely buffet and the race. Lovely day and the following day was our 24th Wedding anniversary. Oh, I hoped that we had turned a bit of a corner. George was happy, I was almost restored to normal, re-energised, full of fun and laughter, tales of our holiday to tell. Simply great.

I had arranged for a bit of an anniversary party at our favourite Indian restaurant, on the Monday evening. George, however, for his own reasons, was not in good humour. He did not want to celebrate and was quite rude. I said to him "come on, we've got our best friends and kids here, let's just have a lovely evening." But he wanted to go home as we had a busy day ahead in the morning. His brain was focused on himself.

George had a Harefield appointment the following day. He did not want me to come with him, why, I do not know, but I insisted, I was not going to let him drive on the M1 and M25 alone. So, an early start and a long drive. George was unpleasant all the way there and even more unpleasant to the staff. I had a quiet word with the doctor whilst George was having blood tests and explained about his mood swings, temper, odd behaviour, going missing, and sort of apologised for his manner. I intimated that both the palliative care consultant, and I, thought there was an element of vascular dementia developing so that they knew what was going on at home. George was insisting once again that he wanted to be admitted to have the valve replaced that was leaking but was told No again. He was really angry when they were adamant that he would not survive the surgery and that it was almost impossible to do it. So, he was very grumpy on the way home, criticizing my driving, saying that I was not fit to be on the road. I thought to myself that the lovely, pleasant happy George of last Sunday had rapidly faded in 2 days and we were back to square one.

Almost Summer
May 29th

The day after the Harefield trip was a day for sorting things out, like the laundry from my holiday and general chores around the house. At lunchtime, I asked George if he had got the HSBC bank statements that I had asked him to get before I went away. He said no, and you can't have them.

Exasperated I replied "I've done your tax returns for the last 25 years, why now are you objecting. What have you got to hide? If you don't give me those statements, I can't complete the tax return. It is the 29th today and the deadline is Friday 31st. Then you will be in arrears. If you don't give me those statements, I will refuse to have anything to do with your tax return ever again, you will have to instruct an accountant, who certainly won't be able to get them in before Friday. Let me take you down to the bank in the village, get the statements, then I can finish the tax return and the job is done. I don't understand what the problem is." Well, we argued about this for the next couple of hours until 3.30pm when George thought the bank would be closed but I knew it didn't shut till 4pm. I eventually got him, still shouting and raving at me, into the car. He refused to put his shoes on so he went in his slippers, grumbling about how he needed a sleep, he was too ill for all this, how I was everything in the world that was cruel, heartless, disputed that my parents were ever married, foul abusive anger for the entire 2 minutes it took to get to the bank. I went in and asked for the statements to be handed over to him. The bank clerk looked at George for his permission and he shouted," Give her the f.....g statements". I felt so sorry for the assistant, she didn't deserve to be spoken to like that, but she printed them off, put them in an envelope and handed them to George. I looked him straight in the face, wondering what on earth all the fuss was about, and took the envelope from him, put it into my handbag and walked out to the car. George shuffled out and got into the passenger seat. I said to him, "That wasn't so painful was it?" he just looked ahead and said nothing. We got home in silence, George went to sit in his chair and put the TV on, it was Countdown and he always liked to watch that programme. I made a pot of tea and took a mug to George with a piece of fruit cake. I took another mug into the office with the envelope and fired up the computer. I said that I wouldn't be many minutes finishing off, I just needed to add the interest payments to the online return and then it would be complete. I don't know what I expected, I knew something was wrong by George's reluctance to give me the statements, but I never expected, in a million years, what came next.

So, I sat down, opened the envelope and read through the sheets of paper and then just stared.

Gobsmacked

Astounded

Horror stuck

Total disbelief at what I saw

I cannot think of adjectives to describe how I felt. Nothing could describe my shock. I felt physically sick, the bottom of my stomach hurt, and I thought my brain was going to explode. Almost in denial I thought, deal with this in a minute, get a hold of yourself, do the job in hand first. So, I methodically added up all the interest earned and added the figures online. When that was done, I read through the whole document making sure there were no mistakes and pressed send. In a nano second HMRC sent a response with the calculation of how much tax was due and when. I pressed print and a few seconds later the printer whirred and spat out 2 sheets of A4 with the relevant information on.

Then I sat and reread the bank statements, over and over and over again.

HSBC Bank Statement Oct – Dec 2012

October 19th, 2012,

payment of £150,000 to Ann

payment of £150,000 to John

What?

£300,000, our pension savings, sale of the development land, gone to George's 2 children.

What?

This was the money earmarked for us to retire with, to keep us, we had very little in the way of a formal pension, always being self-employed, this was what we had to live on for the rest of our lives.

What?

You know when you think things could not ever get any worse, they can. I turned to the next page of the statements

Statement Jan – Mar 2013

February14th, 2013

Payment of £100,000 to Ann

Happy Valentine's Day Elsie!!!

What?

I read it again and again and again. I was shaking inside, from head to toe. When I think back, I wonder to this day how I functioned so relatively normally, or even how I functioned at all.

I sat for a few minutes, in total shock, then walked from the office into the sitting room and handed George the A4 print out of his tax return. Calmly I said "here is the tax return, you need to pay £16,000 (I forget the actual figure and its' irrelevant anyway, but it was £16,000 plus a bit)

It needs to be paid by January 31st, 2014 at the latest or you will incur a penalty charge"

I took a very deep breath as I didn't trust myself to be able to speak at all but as controlled as I could, said "you now know that I know what you have been hiding since October of last year, you have given all our pension savings away to your 2 children. What about all 4 of our children that we promised when we got married to always treat the same? What do you think we are going to live on for the rest of our lives, how are we going to finish the desperately needed renovation to the exterior of the Key House? What on earth were you thinking? Have you completely lost your mind? What you have done is not only illegal, but unfair, immoral and without any discussion with me; we are married, this is our money, you have done this deceitfully and behind my back. Why, what on earth have I ever done for you to lie and cheat like this? For 24 years I have loved you, cared for you, waited hand and foot on you, looked after your businesses, brought your children up. What the hell did you think you were doing and how did you think you would get away with me not finding out about this?"

My controlled speech got less and less controlled as my tirade went on so that by the last sentence, I was almost hysterical.

I stood in front of George's chair and by this time I was visibly shaking, the tears were streaming down my face. I was stunned, devastated, completely shattered. As the realisation started to sink in, I got more distressed. I honestly thought I was going to collapse; I could hardly breathe. George got up out of his chair, looked at me with positive hate, his eyes wild, and hissed " It's my money, I can do what I like with it, you can do nothing about it now but I thought I'd be dead before you found out."

Hanging on to sanity, I replied that I would have to seek legal advice because he had left us both in such a precarious financial state and he retorted by saying, "You won't get a divorce, you are too well looked after and I'm a very sick, terminally ill man. Nobody will take any notice of you. I'm off to bed". With that he got onto his stair lift and went upstairs and got into bed.

I mechanically picked up the tea mugs and plate, went into the kitchen, put the crockery into the dishwasher and sat down, my mind was a total blur. It was just after 4.30 pm. The last hour had totally changed my entire life.

What on earth do I do now? I thought. How can I carry on as if nothing had happened, how can I cook dinner and sit across the table from George? There was no polite conversation I could have. I was in a total turmoil. What was left of our marriage?

I poured a glass of wine, almost on autopilot, and still sat there staring at the wall. I must deal with this, however bad I feel, I must deal with this. Then a blinding flash came over me, we had another joint account, a savings and investment account with The National Farmers Union. Oh, dear god, has he plundered that too? I ran into the office, got the phone number and rang. They confirmed that it was untouched. Thank goodness. I asked if we could change the "either signature to sign" to "joint signatures" as I told them that George was going through a difficult time with his health and I suspected that he was suffering from dementia.

The lady I spoke to was very helpful and asked if I wanted to transfer half the money into an account in my sole name, but I said no, as long as George couldn't take any money out without my knowledge I was happy. Phew. In retrospect, maybe should have transferred the money to my own name, but I was incapable of rational clear thought. I just needed for the money to be held safe.

What to do next? Oh god I needed help.

My trusted friends across the road. Of course. Robert would be able to talk to George. I needed some advice and fast. So, I just wandered across the road, still in total shock, wineglass in hand. Robert was just coming out of his office at that moment, on his way back to the house and in his usual cheery way, kissed me and said," it's no good bringing your glass, where's the rest of the bottle"? starting to laugh. It was the catalyst which woke me out of my nightmare state and I just collapsed in floods of tears. He grabbed my elbow and steered me into the house. Lindsay was in the kitchen, looked at me and said," dear god, whatever's the matter"? I was in such a state I think they both expected me to say that George was dead. Everything that had just happened spilled out of my head, in between uncontrollable sobbing, I relayed what had happened and I think they were as stunned as me. Robert, ever practical, said that I needed legal advice. He rang his corporate lawyer, who I also knew. He confirmed immediately that what George had done was completely illegal but that I needed a family lawyer, not him. It was not his field of expertise but gave us the number of someone who could help. Anyway, he rang this lady lawyer friend and she promised to speak at length to me the following day but told me not to stay in the house.

Robert and Lindsay said that I could stay with them, but I said, thank you, but I would go to my brothers as I had the dog to take care of. Calmer now, but in a dream world, I walked back home, George was snoring, how he could sleep amidst all this trauma I do not know? Over the next half an hour or so, I packed a suitcase of clothes, the dog, dog bed and food and was about to drive off when I had a brain wave. I went back into the office, packed the laptop, all the company accounts, bank statements, car documents, passports, everything appertaining to us, birth and marriage certificates, everything I could find, put it all into a large blue Ikea bag, and off I went to my brother's house. I knew deep down that my marriage was over. There was no going back. How could I?

The following days were a total blur spent at my brother's flat. I phoned the solicitor and had a long talk to her and made an appointment to see her the following Wednesday, no free availability before, I had my hair done on the Friday, just to try and remain normal. I went to see mum and dad to tell them what had transpired; my father was about to go and "deal with George" but at 90, I persuaded him to let me deal with it all. My mother was in tears, my daughter, just having lost little Oscar, went to see George, who had his brother Chris, there to stay. I think, reading between the lines, that they were all very worried about what I was going to do next. Chris was dreadfully rude to Alison but, bless her, she told him to butt out, she had come to talk to George, but she said it was as if George had become another person. The stepfather she knew did not exist anymore. Robert tried to talk to George to no avail either. I rang John. Poor John was due to get married on June 22nd, 3 weeks away. I told John what had transpired. Obviously, he knew about the £150,000 in his bank from the previous October, I suddenly realised that was why he couldn't look me in the face over Xmas, he felt guilty and had been put in a dreadful position, having to keep a secret which he knew in his heart was wrong. What he didn't know was that a further £100,000 had gone to his sister on top of the £150,000. All he could say was "Oh no, immaculate timing Dad!". I told him that I was distraught, I just wanted my life back to normal, but for my own safety I had left the Key House and was having to take legal advice to protect myself. David, who was also dreadfully upset, as I say, all this trauma coming 2 months after the death of little Oscar, tried to talk to Ann, to no avail. We were all still grieving, it was just a living nightmare. I think David would have liked to have got hold of George and given him a right ear bashing, but I dissuaded him. It was all too raw.

Monday 3rd June. I rang our bank manager who had looked after all our affairs for years. I asked if I could go to see him as I needed to talk over some things with him. He was going to come to the house, but I said I would prefer to go to his office. I saw him the following day at 10am. He was shocked and horrified at what I told him, but he put his business hat on and sorted out a new bank account for me and transferred half of our joint current account into the new one, arranged for my state pension money to go into the new one and left the old joint one for George to use. I had a dormant account that I had used for the kids when they were at university so I could put their allowance money in for them to draw out with their own cash cards. We revived that account as my main one to use from now on. We had a small saving account with just £8,000 in it. The bank manager suggested I transferred that into my sole name. I was reluctant to do this, but he just raised his eyebrows and said to me gently, "George has just defrauded you out of £400,000 of money and you are worried about £8K". He said that I was going to need it to instruct a lawyer and I had got to live. I needed a fighting fund. So, I agreed.

June 5th, I met my lawyer. What a wonderful lady whom I will never forget. She was my guiding light over the next few months and don't think I would be here today without her help. She will be known as R in this story from now on. She listened to my tale of woe and said of all the cases she had ever dealt with, this was the worst, the most distressing and cruel she had ever heard. A barrister friend of hers had called in, on the off chance of a coffee break, and R asked her to come in for some advice. I sat in her office shaking, in tears, absolutely sobbing my heart out, saying I did not want a divorce, I just wanted my life, as it used to be, back again. The light bulb moment came when the barrister gently said, kneeling down beside me and taking my hands, "please tell me why you want to remain married to a man who can lie and cheat and treat you like that after all the years you have done absolutely everything for him, nursed him through critical medical crises, stood by him through thick and thin, run the businesses and brought up his children. Then he blatantly and deliberately deceives you out of nearly half a million pounds of your own hard-earned money and legally changed the ownership of your home and investment property. Just tell me why?"

I sat up straight, looked her in the eyes, heartbroken, scared of what I was going to say next and sadly I said, "I don't. I need my dignity and self-respect back. I feel like an abused victim and I do not want to be a victim anymore. I know how ill he is, but I cannot go on living like this."

I honestly believe that, even now, 7 years later, I know I have my self-respect back, I have my dignity back, but I still feel traumatised. It is making me cry just writing this and recalling it all. I felt as if I had been used, made to feel inadequate, under his control, trampled on, trodden into the ground and I knew I would have to summon every ounce of strength and courage to fight back. Where I got it from, I do not know, but I did. Almost.

I digress, I need to write this as it is the only way I think I will ever put the past behind me. I must get it out of myself somehow to free myself from the trauma.

That same day, George went to see his solicitor, who had acted for us both in the past, was our friend as well as our lawyer. He told George that he was not a divorce lawyer, had a conflict of interests as he had previously been my friend as well as our joint lawyer, so advised him to get another firm of solicitors to act for him.

I had, with my legal advice, been told to return home but to sleep in a separate bedroom. Well I certainly was not going to sleep with him again was I? So, I moved my things and the dog back home and into the spare bedroom. I had asked all 4 of our children to come around at 5pm that evening to have a family pow wow. Armed with my legal rights and position, I was able to stand, head held high and conduct myself with power and knowledge. I laid my cards on the table, said that as I knew how sick George was and John's impending wedding, I wanted no more drama, no more lies and deceit. If Ann and John would repay all the money back into our joint names and George would arrange to put our properties back into joint names, we could put all this behind us, start again and rebuild our family and our lives. Ann would not come, said it was too far to drive and didn't want to see me anyway, she did not agree with me, did not accept that her dad had done anything wrong and was very abusive to me. But the other 3 kids met. It was all very frosty and uncomfortable. John shuffled around with his head hung so he wouldn't meet any of our eyes and said nothing. I said that I didn't want a divorce but I had to protect myself so things had to be put right, or I would be going ahead. George was convinced in his somewhat addled brain that I was not going to get anything, that a judge would take pity on his poor health, so absolutely refused my requests. After that abortive meeting I was left with no choice. It was my last-ditch effort to save my marriage and the unity of our family.

It wasn't to be.

June 6th, I rang R and said we must go ahead with the divorce. My last efforts had failed, and I could not allow this to drag on any longer. She agreed and we arranged to go to the court to register the divorce, pulling some strings to get the case heard very quickly as George was so ill. We were lucky enough to have a brief meeting with the judge who agreed that speed was of the essence because of Georges state of health. He said to me that he would have granted me a divorce on a quarter of the evidence I had submitted. He granted the divorce on the grounds of unreasonable behaviour and mental cruelty, there and then. It was the fastest divorce ever to take place in Leicestershire. Next, the Judge wanted the financial settlement to be dealt with as quickly as possible and instructed a date as soon as Court time could be arranged.

George was completely shocked when he received the divorce papers. I was there when he opened the post and went white. I do not think he really thought I would go through with it. Stunned, he immediately checked himself into hospital. Hospital was, in his mind, like a comfort blanket. He could hide there and use his illness as an escape. I took him in, and he then told John he wouldn't be going to the wedding. That was emotional blackmail as obviously John wanted his dad to be there on his most important day; I suggested to John that I should back out to as I did not want his special day blighted by our traumas. I didn't want to see George's ex-wife, his daughter, his brother and certainly didn't want a bad atmosphere on this very special day. He said that no, he wanted me there, I had been a big and important part of his life, and I had always been very fond of him, so I agreed to be there. It was to be up in the north of Derbyshire, at an hotel in the Peak District, so I arranged a family room that slept 4 for the night before and the night of the wedding, mainly so that Alison and Carl could stay with me. David was already attending a friend's wedding in Italy, which had been arranged before John had booked the same date. George was still in hospital, but Ann prevailed on him to come so, she picked him up in the morning from hospital and I took his suit and necessary clothing, had his Bentley washed and valeted for the occasion and the wedding proceeded without a hitch and was a lovely day. The sun shone, the venue was beautiful, and I stayed out of the way as much as possible from the family.. The atmosphere however, between Chris,

George's brother and me, was icy, he said, behind my back, but loud enough for me to hear, that I looked like a tart. Well I did not. I wore a lovely navy lace dress, with a pretty fascinator, keeping it classy and discreet. I have never looked like a tart in my life, but he was just being as unpleasant as he could be because his plans had been rumbled and thwarted. The tension between us all was palpable but for John' sake we were all well behaved. Ben and Ann were friendly enough with Alison and Carl during the day, but Ben said privately to Carl that he didn't understand what all the fuss was about. Why had I got so upset about this amount of money? "George has got stacks of money; I don't get why this small amount given away has caused such havoc and an impending divorce". Carl looked him straight in the face and said "Mate, you don't understand, this is virtually all the money there is, Alison's mum will be left penniless and homeless if George dies, there's no other money" Ben was speechless, obviously having been led to beleive that we were worth far more than we were, and he hadn't grasped the fact that I would be not own my own home and with no savings if and when George died. Looking at George then, he looked as if he was not going to last much longer. He was so painfully thin, grey pallor, his suit looked as if it was 3 sizes too big; he just looked so sad but quite wild eyed as if he did not comprehend what was going on in his life. Just a sad, confused old man. I wanted to put my arms round him but knew I could not do it anymore. Ben started to understand the gravity of the situation.

George had self-discharged himself but had promised to get back to the hospital after the wedding. Well that was never going to happen as, after a few glasses of fizz, Ann did not want to drive all the way back, about an hour and a half's drive away. I certainly was not going to take him; Chris was drunk and abusive so there was no choice but for George to stay in my family room. He slept in the twin room, Alison and Carl had the double and I had the put you up sofa. I took George back home to the Key House the following day; the hospital would not have him back as he had not returned as arranged the night before, thus depriving another patient a bed for the night. It seemed as if the nightmare would never end.

Summer

The days after John's wedding were odd, word had got out amongst local friends, motor racing circles and wider family. I, in a spirit of defiance, went about my social life alone, trying to put a brave face on things and stiff upper lip. I went to the British GP, Doghouse meetings, Tangent gatherings, a friends' 60th birthday party, the local Conservative Summer Lunch "do", Mandy and Peters' son's, wedding, annual Music in the Park event in the village, Robert and Lindsay's great party and County Show. It was hot and sunny, I had lost loads of weight (divorce is always good for a loss of a stone or 2) so I tried to look as good as I could, all self defence mechanisms. I would stay out late and never say where I was going or who with. I know that it upset George hugely, but I was not trying to get revenge, I was far too hurt inside (and still am really). I am not sure what it was that drove me on, but I think that the more I did and became involved in, the less time I had to take in the enormity of what had happened.

The Judge, at the court hearing, had asked me if I wanted to stay in the Key House to which I replied in the negative. I told him that I had never wanted to live there in the first place, it was far too big for me and far too expensive to run and it also still needed a lot of renovation work which would be at huge cost. So, the judge had told me to start looking for somewhere to rent until the money could be sorted out. I had looked at a few properties over the previous couple of weeks knowing full well that I would have to move again.

July 19th The Judge had set another court hearing a few weeks later after John had returned from honeymoon. I am not sure how they managed to enjoy it knowing that they had to face court when they returned home. He ordered Ann and John to attend along with George. David and Alison wanted to come with me for support, but I said no. It would have been dreadful sitting in the court room with the split families looking across the table at each other, brothers and sisters torn apart. I said I would rather keep it calm, quiet and dignified. I did not want, and could not have coped with, the possibility of a slanging match. So, I sat quietly in the court with my solicitor. George was there with his brother, solicitor, Ann, her barrister and John, who just hung his head. Weirdly, George had asked if he could take my car, the Evoque and I could drive the Bentley. I thought it a bit odd but said yes, I loved driving the Bentley anyway so took my solicitor to the court and we arrived in style!. Then of course we found out why George wanted my car. He couldn't get his Motability scooter in the Bentley and he wanted to appear in court looking as disabled and pathetic as possible. All another contrived plot.

The Judge opened the proceedings, George thought that by attending on his Motability scooter, the judge would think that I was the big, bad ogre. He was stunned by the opposite being the case. The judge saw straight though that. The event went in a blur, it was absolutely dreadful, the judge was, of course, totally impartial and fair but wonderful and afterwards I left felt vindicated and that justice had been done.

1. I was asked to leave the Key House and find somewhere to rent

2. George was to pay me £3000 per month maintenance until the financial settlement was complete: George was aghast and shouted, "I can't afford that". The judge quietly said that he should have thought about that before he started giving our money away.

3. John was ordered to pay back the £150,000 within 7 days, to his solicitor, which he agreed to do immediately.

4. Ann was ordered to pay £250,000 back under the same terms. Oh wow, that did not go down well. Understatement! Her barrister said that she could not pay back the money. It was revealed that she had paid the £100,000, that had been transferred on Valentine's day, to her mother in a Spanish bank account. Oh, so she had been part of the plot as well. Well, well! The judge ordered that to be repaid immediately or Susan would face consequences too. John just shook his head in disbelief. The barrister agreed to get that money back but said it would take a bit of time to get it back from Tenerife. The

other £150,000 was not able to be repaid as it had all been spent. Even I, sat like a little mouse, gasped. The judge was horrified and said "you mean that since last October you have spent £150,000? What on? You will provide evidence of the spending. Ann said that she had paid off part of her mortgage, had bought her and her husband a new Mercedes each and new Rolex watches, money for her daughter, a car for her husband's nephew, holidays and new clothes. Oh, she had been on a mega spending spree.

The Judge was, to put it very mildly, not at all impressed at all and said that Ann had better raise a mortgage on her flat in order to repay the money. She shrieked and said that as they were both out of work they couldn't get a mortgage. These were outright lies as Ann worked for a London Estate Agent and Ben had a property development company. The judge then said that she would have to sell the flat to repay the money, to which Ann burst into floods of tears. He said, "you are just not taking this seriously, you do not realise what you have done. None of you have realised what you have done. This money did not belong to your father. It belonged to both your father and stepmother. In any long term marriage there is no "his or hers" money. It belongs jointly to them both. Your stepmother knew nothing about what had been done and did not give permission for this to be given away. It was illegal and the amount we are talking about, in law, is termed as Grand Theft.. It carries a custodial sentence and you will go to jail if this money is not repaid. This amount would carry an 18 month sentence. Phew that brought the whole courtroom alive. After a couple of seconds of absolute silence, the eruptions on the other side of the table started. Ann's barrister rose to his feet and objected, Ann shouted that it was her dad's money and he could give away whatever he liked, but she was white and shaking. George was also as white as a sheet but said nothing. The judge quietly spoke to George asking him what had possessed him to do what he had done, not only over the money but over the will and property transactions as well. Why, to a wife of 24 years who had cared for him and looked after him through all his dreadful health issues. A faithful, loving and caring wife. He just replied saying that his daughter and brother had advised him badly, had told him that I had stolen over £200,000 and had been having an affair. George said that over the change to his will was to protect his children from being disinherited by me after his death. He didn't realise the ramifications on me being impoverished by the wording.

5. The judge asked me if I had a recent copy of my will and I said yes, and R, my solicitor, handed it over to him. Of course it was the original will as I had not been able to change it, the identical ones we had made together, made when George and I had got married where we said that we would each leave the other everything we had, whichever of us died first, then when we had both died the money would be divided equally between all four of our children. The judge just raised his eyebrows and said that George should have discussed the change to his will with me and not his brother. The judge then asked me to account for the £200,000 I was

supposed to have stolen. I was prepared for this and produced the list of expenditure. (Remember the list of expenditure from 2012). George just hung his head, drained and just said that his brother had been responsible for the whole plan, (plot), and had advised him badly. He said that Chris had convinced him that I (me) had stolen over £200,000 and was having an affair.

The judge looked me straight in the face and reminded me that I was, like everyone there, under oath. "did you ever have an affair, or give your husband cause to think that you were deceiving him?" What!!! "No" I replied "I would never do that. My husband and I have been through some traumas during our lives together. I have cared for him for 22 of our 24 years. It would never in a million years occur to me to do that.

The judge said that it was not bad advice that Chris had given. It was a deliberate case of attempted fraud, greed and jealousy. George looked ghastly; he was absolutely stunned. John never looked up from the floor.

6. The Judge said that he wanted a 15-minute comfort break before reaching his decisions as fraud and grand theft was a very serious offence and he wanted to consider the sentence.

7. I left the court with my solicitor first and went into a side room. My mouth was desperately dry. I had no idea that the Judge would consider a jail sentence and I said that I could not see my stepdaughter go to jail, for that happen to any of my family and

my granddaughter, in particular, who was only 16. It would be awful for her to see her mother go to jail. I had no idea what was happening in another side room, but R said that she was certain that an offer to settle would be sent very quickly before we went back into the courtroom. Of course, she was right. A few minutes passed and a runner came in, handed in a piece of handwritten paper with an offer to settle. R looked at it and we went through it carefully, she said that it was not fair as it didn't take into consideration the money that had already been given away, so we rewrote it asking for at least half of the original value of the estate before the money was given away. It was sent back with the phrase that no further counteroffers would be acceptable. We would just go back into court and let the judge decide. They agreed just as the bell sounded for us to go back in.

8. George's solicitor told the Judge that a financial settlement had been agreed in order to prevent a jail sentence. The Judge was very pleased, (and I think very relieved) with the outcome; that I had already been granted a divorce on the grounds of mental cruelty and unreasonable behaviour and had received the offer of an almost just settlement He then ordered George to pay my costs, ouch, he didn't like that and started to object, but that was turned down. Ann's barrister asked for her costs and that was greeted with "how dare you even ask" and I was awarded a further £1000 costs from Ann.

You would really have called it a result, but it didn't feel like it. It was almost a just and fair one, but I felt physically and emotionally drained. I went home feeling incredibly sad that life as I had known it for 25 years was well and truly over. Worse, I went home to see George sitting in his chair, defiant but utterly defeated.

What a sad chapter I have just written. Chris and Ann had so much to answer for, plotting through greed and the cause of such a tragedy to all our lives.

NEW START?

July 24th, Ann, who thought she knew better than all the expert cardiologists at Harefield Hospital, found a heart surgeon in London who thought he could mend George's leaking valve, so she collected George and took him to this private clinic in the centre of London. Lord knows how much that cost! I had the Key House to myself, which for a few days was wonderfully peaceful. I was looking hard for a property to rent but everything I looked at was either too big, too small or in the wrong place and I was getting a bit worried about finding something. I had registered on Right Move for both rent and sale and on the morning of 24th, George had only just left when a property for sale was reduced in price, so it popped into my inbox. I phoned immediately for an appointment; I could see from the photographs that it was empty so might be available for rent too. I went to view that afternoon and I knew, as we drove through the security gates, that I had found my forever home. I knew before even walking through the door. It was a mile and a half outside the village, it was out in the countryside, it was far enough away from George, secret enough for him not to know where I was, yet near enough to friends and the village. It was all on one level, a barn conversion in a courtyard of just 4, a private walled garden, hidden from the rest of the world, it had 3 bedrooms; it was just perfect. By 3pm I had asked the agent to ask the owner if I could put in an offer but rent whilst the sale went through. After some phone calls back and forth, by 6pm I had done the deal.

25th I met the owner at the house; he was a serving Army officer about to go back from leave so wanted everything sorting out before he left. I truthfully told him my sad saga and he was happy for me to pay him rent till the sale could complete. I was absolutely honest and said that the divorce settlement had been agreed, but it would take a couple of months for the money to be sorted and in my account; we relied on each other in trust and I paid him 4 months' rent in cash there and then as proof and his solicitor had sent a rental agreement for me to sign. By lunchtime I had the keys and we had shaken hands on the deal. I went off to the hairdresser, then straight to Silverstone for the annual Classic Meeting, stayed overnight, came home the following day and prepared food for the Conservative Summer Lunch on the Sunday.

29th I had arranged for my cleaning ladies to come in and blitz the house clean. It was not in bad shape, just dusty from standing empty since February, so with bathrooms cleaned, floors mopped and kitchen degreased, I was ready for the big move. I was desperate to move before George came home from hospital. I had no idea where he was or what procedures had been arranged but I did not want him at the Key House (no longer home to me) when I moved out. It would just have been too stressful for us both.

30th and 31st One of my closest friends, Colleen, volunteered to help and she and I moved lots of kitchen and bathroom stuff so that I could be up and running quickly, there is nothing worse than moving house and not being able to find the kettle and mugs to make tea or not be able to have a bath or shower. I arranged the removal company to come in on 31st and moved whatever furniture I wanted. In fact, I didn't take too much as the new house was much smaller and the existing dining room and sitting room furniture was just too big. I took the spare bedroom furniture, wardrobes, beds and everything I would need initially. We had so much china, glass, linen etc. that I was able to leave the Key House for George intact with fresh bedding and towels, complete dining room and sitting room, I took one of the 2 dinner services, one of the two sets of cutlery, garden furniture; basically divided the house into two. By the end of the day almost everything I wanted was in the new house and the cleaning ladies came in to make the Key House look clean and tidy after the removals. I spent my last night at the Key House as I was so keen to get everything I wanted out and get the house looking as normal as possible for George that I hadn't had chance to unpack at the new house. I was terrified that he might arrive home whilst I was mid move. I wanted to be in control of the move and out before he returned.

Officially I took up residence at my new home on 1st August 2013.

I need not have worried; George did not come home for a further week. As previously predicted, the doctors at the private hospital had deliberated over George's condition, liaised with the consultants at Harefield and agreed that the valve replacement surgery was just not possible, far too dangerous to undertake and sent him home. So much for Ann's "expertise" in the field of George's heart condition. I've no idea how much that private hospital cost to give the same diagnosis that Harefield had given us over a year previously.

George was horrified when he came home to find that I had moved out. Somewhere in his brain, I do not think he really thought I would go. He was very, very distressed, kept phoning my mobile asking where I was. I went down to see him, to make sure he was ok, arranged for carers to come in for him and got the cleaning ladies booked in to regularly go in to clean, change bedding, towels, laundry etc.

THE BEGINNING OF MY NEW LIFE

It was a few days of euphoria, the move was, although stressful, exciting, getting the new house arranged and unpacked, working out how the heating worked, telephone engineers, tv connections, family and friends visiting to see where I was. The summer of 2013 was a particularly hot one, so the doors were open all day, I spent a lot of time outside designing my new garden and getting used to the total peace and calm of my new life. The quiet was almost deafening. After all the traumas and difficulties of the past few years, there was no one shouting at me, no one demanding things of me, no whizzing between hospital appointments, doctors' visits, consultants, carers, pill management, cooking 3 meals a day. No demands on my time at all. I could lie in or get up as I pleased. Sometimes I deliberately didn't cook a meal because I didn't have to have dinner on the table every night. I could go out without having to explain where I was going, who I was seeing and what time I would be back. I was, for the first time in 25 years, my own person. I was ME again.

It gave me time to reflect, remember, be sad, cry, grieve for my little lost grandson, for myself, for the loss of my life as I had known it, for my shattered marriage and family but also to be joyful, be able to smile at the prospect of being free. So many conflicting emotions.

Sometimes I felt very guilty, as if I had abandoned my responsibility to George. I knew from close friends that he wasn't doing very well; he wasn't going to be, was he? He had lost his lifelong support system (me) and had to start fending for himself. He didn't really do it for himself. I, with support, had organised everything for him. I took him to the co-op so he could do his shopping, took him to get his hair cut, a friend would call in for coffee to make sure he was ok, Robert and another good friend Tony, took him out for his birthday lunch on 15th August. Where were his family? Where was Chris? Well after the money had all been recalled there wasn't any need to come and see him, anymore was there? The cash had all been awarded to me to buy my own house, George kept the Key House and his private pension; there wasn't anything else the family could get their hands on, so they all faded away. John visited from time to time, probably once a week to take George a Chinese Take Away but essentially it was his close friends and me that kept him going.

THE END OF 2013

Alison and Carl had to move out of their rented house as the landlord wanted to put it up for sale. The two of them, still shell shocked from the loss of little Oscar and the complete fiasco and tragedy of my situation, Alison's loss of her so-called stepfather, stepbrother and sister, just the whole family torn in half, made them stop and take stock. I suggested that they took themselves off on an extended holiday, so they moved out of the house, everything went into storage and they bought flights to New Zealand, just took off on 20th August. Their cats moved in with me and off they went to clear their heads and work out how to start their lives all over again.

I had to go back to court twice during September as George was refusing to pay maintenance until the divorce money went through, the Judge was completely exasperated with him, but slowly, slowly it dawned on him that he had to comply. He tried very hard to find out where I was but my friends, bless their hearts, never let on to him that they knew where I was living and to my eternal gratitude, he never did find me. He never set foot in this house so there is no memory or ghost of him here.

I kept terribly busy, learning to live by myself, was off out to friends; I became a social butterfly. The Doghouse Ladies, the Tangent girls, Silverstone with racing friends, always out and about, with no restraints anymore; It was as if I had been set free and let out.

Whilst I was physically set free, emotionally and

mentally I was wrecked. The devastation refused to leave me; in truth it never has done to this day although I am much better now. I would wake up in the night, sometimes I found myself with tears streaming down my face, sometimes it was a nightmare, sometimes I could not sleep at all, other times I would sleep so soundly it would be 9 or 10 am when I woke. I was not settled; I was not calm. Still no inner peace. It was a sort of hysteria, life and soul of the party whilst out with friends but a basket case on my own at night. I still ask myself even now, how the hell did it happen, how did I have my eye so off the ball, must have been total complacency and, most crucially, why? What on earth had I done to deserve it?

I haven't said much recently about David, but without fuss, he was here for me at all times, very supportive whilst having his own emotional crisis due the loss of his family as he knew it and seeing Alison in such a state and at odds with their real father too.. Quietly he got on with his life but was always at the end of the phone for me. We had a curry together or a steak every now and then and whilst Alison was away we kept close. Obviously he was worried about his mother and sisters state's of mind.

So, the autumn approached, September came and went then Alison and Carl came home. They moved in with me temporarily, much refreshed and in a better place emotionally. They went house hunting and found a new house to buy and so I felt happier that they were getting their lives back on track.

21st October. Whopping great setback, with no warning at all the Decree Nisi finally arrived by post. Of course, I knew it was coming but nevertheless when you look at a sheet of paper just saying that your marriage is over, it came as a devastating blow. 24 years of my life wiped away by a sheet of paper. The destruction, the hurt and the emotion, all came rushing back over me like a tsunami. I might have looked OK and is if I was coping well but you didn't have to scratch the surface very far to see the dithering wreck below.

I knew that I was in dire need of a break. With Alison, Carl and David quite settled, I now needed to get away and give myself some time out. I booked a cruise going from Southampton on November 17th. I was extremely nervous about going away completely by myself. It took a lot of courage that I didn't have, to drive down to Southampton and get on a ship, completely alone, I'd done this journey many times over the past few years but even though George was a sick man and I had had to do everything for him, it was still someone with you. Still had my husband to talk to. Still had my dignity and self-confidence. Not any more time to do this alone,

Sometimes, however, you simply do not realise how lucky you are. As I boarded ship, I got to my cabin and was about to unpack when a couple of cabin stewards arrived and told me that my cabin had been changed, please would I follow them, and they would bring all my luggage. I was taken up 2 deck levels where I found that my cabin had been upgraded to a balcony suite with, roses, chocolates, champagne, canapes and a fruit bowl. Wow, then an invitation arrived to meet the Captain for a drink before dinner. I had not realised that one of our friends, who had bought one of our barn conversions some years before, was this ships' Captain. Oh, he made the holiday so good for me. I enjoyed myself thoroughly and can never thank Neil enough. I came home feeling calmer and able to think a little more calmly about what life ahead was going to be like. I met some lovely people on board, I laughed, rested, swam, had massages, explored, walked and shopped; the whole experience did me a huge amount of good.

Life in my new house started to take on a structure; there was lots to do, like painting and decorating, furniture to buy, where to put things, what I needed, what I didn't need! George had moved into the annex to the Key House and had rented the main house out. I had a phone call from him every day asking for my help. Could I take him to the chemist, the Co-Op, the doctors, could I do the washing, food shopping, cooking, bank statements he didn't understand; the list went on. Every day without fail, he needed me for something, I went down most days and took him meals, organised the cleaning ladies for him; I pretty much did what I had been doing all my married life for him. His mind was very evidently becoming more addled, he couldn't remember why he had phoned me or even that he had phoned me at all. Slowly, I got carers, cleaners, doctors, chemist deliveries, food deliveries, all sorted out for him, but he still phoned me, every day. He couldn't understand why I had divorced him, still couldn't take in what he had done wrong. His brain was going, and the dementia was taking over. He didn't recognise people, got irritable (more than usual) and the frustration within him must have been dreadful.

Life started to take on a pattern of its' own, friends and family were wonderful, and slowly I started to rebuild myself quietly.

2013 had not quite finished with me though. Just when

you think that all the dreadful things in the world that had been thrown at you were over, there was another curved ball about to swipe me sideways.

Sunday lunch in early December was spent at the local pub with my brother and mum and dad. It had become a regular date which I enjoyed hugely. We used to take a friend of my parents out to lunch with us as she was a widow and did not get much of a social life. I went home about 3pm. About 5 o'clock the phone rang. It was dad in a bit of a state. Could I come over quickly as mum had collapsed in the kitchen. Dad had caught her and got her onto a chair, but she wasn't making any sense. He didn't dare let go of her in case she fell. So, I told Dad that I was on my way but first I phoned 999 as I suspected a stroke, then phoned Henry and drove straight over to their house. The ambulance, Henry and I pretty much all got there at the same time. Mum was conscious but couldn't speak or co-ordinate movements, so she was stretchered, for her own safety, and off we went, Dad and I in the Ambulance and Henry followed by car. Some 4 hours later, having negotiated Accident and Emergency, mum was admitted to the Stroke Unit in Derby, exactly where I had been with George a couple of years previously. Henry and I got Dad home, he didn't want to leave Mum, but it was late, and he was tired. I arranged to pick him up the following afternoon to visit. Dad was exhausted so I told him to have a lie in and I knew Mum would be in for a barrage of scans and tests. The following day it was confirmed that it was a stroke although no permanent damage done. Mum spent 2 weeks in hospital then came home to recuperate. Her movement came back slowly but she was able to manage with a lot of help from Dad. Her speech took longer, and she got very frustrated with herself because she knew what she wanted to say but the words just would not come out of her mouth. Exactly like George. As I remember saying to him, it was a bit like déjà vu; having a stroke is a bit like being in a library where all the books used to be in alphabetical order, so you knew exactly where to find things, but then an earthquake shakes all the books onto the floor. They are all still there but in the wrong order, all in a heap so you can't find what you are looking for. Recovering is like slowly putting those books back on the shelf, in the right place. I do not underestimate just how hard that can be. I am not attributing blame here, but I think poor mum had seen her daughter and granddaughter suffer dreadfully together with the distress of losing Oscar and had caused her stress level to reach heights that she couldn't deal with anymore and that caused the stroke.

Like life, when things catastrophically change, slowly you adapt to a new way of doing things and it carries on. So by Christmas I was determined to have a great family event, to put behind us the year that had almost gone and celebrate that, although all of us were changed and damaged for ever, we had survived and would find strength within ourselves and our family to cope and rebuild ourselves.

Christmas was a good one, I went totally over the top with decorations, presents and food, everyone enjoyed it and I was ready to say good riddance to 2013. What a year!.

New Year's Eve was a different matter altogether. Friends had persuaded me to join them for dinner to a local restaurant, despite my misgivings. I wasn't looking forward to it at all even though the best thing to do was to say goodbye to 2013, I just couldn't face it so I agreed to go but said I would leave by 11.45 at the latest. Sadly, the place was rammed with people and I just could not get out in time. As the clock struck midnight, I ran, tears streaming down my face, I just couldn't handle Auld Lang Syne. It was my breaking point. I got home and just put my head under the duvet and howled. I howled for little Oscar, for George, for my destroyed marriage, my torn apart family, life as I had known it, for myself and for my Mum. I just let it all out, it was long overdue.

2014

I am getting to the end of the saga, but I must complete the story. I thought that 2014 would be the fresh start that I had not wanted but now had to have.

It wasn't the peaceful year that I hoped it would be. It had some highs and lows but at least, mentally, I was beginning to get stronger and more able to cope. One of the defining moments was, that I realised that from now on, I would not be surprised by anything anymore. I also realised that it would be a very long time, if ever, that I would trust anyone again. I think that the events of 2013 had desensitised me and even though 2014 was going to chuck some more things at me, nothing has ever quite come close to the devastation of 2013.

January

Mum managed to dislocate her hip – again. That is the third time, so back she went into hospital for 10 days. Dad, now almost 91, looked at me with despair in his eyes. We were at mum's bedside and I could see what he was thinking." She's not yet recovered from a stroke and how the hell am I going to deal with the practicalities of looking after her now, how to shower her, how to cook?" I looked at Dad, his shoulders slumped, and the light gone out of his eyes. "Dad I think you and mum should start to think about….". He interrupted me saying "going into an old people's home". "No Dad, I would like you and Mum to discuss between you about coming to live with me, I have a 3 bedroomed house, all on the flat, no stairs. We can arrange carers to come in to help. You would need to think about selling your house and you cannot come till the summer as I am facing hip surgery in February and I have booked a month in the South of France in May. Talk to mum and see what you think. "I don't remember ever seeing my Dad cry, but the tears just streamed down his face, lots of them. The relief that his burden could be shared, that help was at hand, was palpable. "Kid, you don't know what you have just said" through muffled sobs he replied. Quick as a flash and to diffuse the emotion I said "oh, Dad I do, and I'm regretting it already" at which we both laughed. It amazes me how you can laugh and cry at the same time. Anyway, I took dad home and said I would pick him up to go back to the hospital the following afternoon. When I arrived at their house the next day, a For Sale sign was on the gate. I was astonished "Dad you didn't discuss that for long" I said. He replied," we didn't need to ". And that was that.

February

Saw Mum home but with lots of help in the home, and preparations for the move, new beds and chairs arranged, my hip surgery was postponed and rebooked.

March

Surgery rescheduled for March 12th. Unfortunately, I had booked a Driving Experience at Donington Park Racing Circuit for David's 40th birthday, his birthday had been on January 9th but the first date I could book was March 14th, catering and hospitality for his friends and family were all arranged. Where was I? In the Nuffield Hospital recovering.

Everyone came in afterwards to tell me what a great day they had enjoyed. David was nominated driver of the day; I wonder where he had learned those driving skills from? But he had thoroughly enjoyed himself which was what mattered most. Hmm!! I came home and spent the next 5 weeks learning to walk again. I found it difficult to make a cup of tea, and carry it, using crutches. Not just difficult, impossible, but it gave me the incentive to use one walking stick, which I did quickly. The weather was good, so I walked a little more down the lane every day and soon got a level of fitness back. My wonderful orthopaedic surgeon, Peter, and great friend of many years had said that if I could walk into the Nuffield without any sticks at all after 5 weeks then I could go on my pre-arranged drive to France. I was determined to go. My Eurotunnel ticket was booked, hotels along the way, Bennion had his dog passport and my brother said he would come with me to share the drive

April 29th

Henry, Bennion and I went off on our French adventure. Peter said that he was a bit concerned about the long drive and made me promise not to drive longer than 2 hours at a time, then walk around for at least 20 minutes then swap drivers. So that is what we did. I meticulously planned the route. My wonderful friends from Florida, quite by chance, were in France on holiday and were at Giverny to visit Monet's garden on the 1st day we were driving down so we arranged to meet them at the ship they were cruising on.

I had plotted the route and I did the first stint from the Eurotunnel, then after a coffee stop, Henry took the wheel.

He was happy to drive but had stipulated that we were not to drive through Paris. I told him the route was organised, so when he said "sis, you told me we were not going anywhere near Paris" I replied that we were nowhere near, "what's that then, look out of the window, it's the bloody Eiffel Tower" Oops, he's never let me forget that either. We met up with G and Mary Anne, had to retell all the horror of the year before but they have stayed great friends with me, very understanding and lovely people. They were so very sad to hear what I had gone through and so sorry about the state of George's mind, but G understood that Heart Transplants, heart disease and strokes can alter personalities and onset of dementia can cause devastation. We had a few hours with them, then I tackled Monet's Garden with my walking stick. I was determined to walk round but I was in a lot of pain after. The rest of the journey down was lovely, stopping off in Beaune and Avignon on the way. I was determined to spend the month getting fit again, mending both my body and my mind. I love the South of France, the apartment in Villefranche was familiar, having been there many times before. Henry stayed for a few days then flew back home. I walked, met old racing friends there for the Historic Meeting and the Monaco Grand Prix, enjoyed the warm sun, the total distraction from the last 12 months, the sea air and slowly I mended my myself.

May 27th

would, and should, have been my 25th Wedding Anniversary. The Silver one.

Cast your mind back if you can to January 2013 when

I had planned a wonderful trip of a lifetime for George and me on the Orient Express from Paris to Venice to celebrate. Fortunately, I had managed to cancel that and get the deposit back, but in my head, although we were now divorced, I still felt that it was an important milestone to mark - or should have been!

Before I left for France, I had composed a letter to George, not an unpleasant letter, but to mark the date of what should have been a momentous occasion, one I had planned and saved for, but of course, with what had happened, all to no avail. I had left the letter with Robert and Lindsay asking them to take it over to George on the 27th, which they did. With great trepidation, not knowing the content of the letter, they deliberated as to which of them would take it but in the end they took it over to George together and ran back home before he could open it.

Having spent a lovely month in the warm sunshine, walking on the beach, reading books, even doing some painting and sketching, healing my hip and my heart, on the 27th I decided to treat myself to lunch at my favourite restaurant in the world. The Chevre d'Or in Eze, perched high up on the top of the cliff overlooking the Mediterranean Sea, lunch on the terrace was a wonderful place to celebrate. George and I had gone there numerous times in the past for our wedding anniversary. The Maître "D" recognised me at once, "ou et George, Madam Elsie." I replied, "divorce". "Non" he uttered, "Oui" I answered "avez vous une table pour moi sur le terrasse avec le petit chien, Bennion?". "Bien sur. Du champagne?" I do like to practice my awfully bad, schoolgirl French whenever I can. Within seconds I was sat at a table on the terrace, a bowl of water for Bennion and a glass of rose champagne in my hand. My toast to myself was "I have survived the horrors of 2013 and, on what should have been a wonderful milestone day, I am in the glorious sunshine, in my favourite restaurant in the South of France, and George is at home, lonely and miserable. Not a gloat or a triumph, more that I had survived, battle weary and sad but that I was ok.

Onwards and upwards. Here is to Love, Lies, Life, Cheers".

I drove back after a delicious and monumentally expensive lunch, stopped off at the antique fair in Beaulieu and bought myself a vintage Tiffany silver necklace. Perfect, a silver present to myself. As I drove into the garage at the apartment my mobile phone rang. It was George. He had read the letter and was in tears. I told him that I didn't want my day spoiling and that I would talk to him when I was back home in a few days' time. The letter had hit home.

27th May 2014

Dear George

As today would have been our Silver Wedding Anniversary, I felt that I could not let the date pass without some sort of recognition.

25 years of marriage would have been a huge milestone to have celebrated and I would have reflected that between us we managed to raise 4 very lovely children without any major catastrophes along the way. We managed, despite your serious health issues, to have, on the whole, a very good marriage. We went to some lovely places, had some extremely good times, some very difficult times through your health but we overcame them together. We moved house a lot, 11 times as I recall, but each time we made a great home and had a good standard of living. We had good friends, a supportive family and together we made a good team.

The past 18 months, however, have made me realise that I was living under a cloud of evil deception. It is now completely obvious that you did not love me at all, if ever. You used me to provide full time care for you and during that time plotted and schemed to disinherit me. I kept house, did all the books and paperwork, dealt with your tax returns and arranged all the household affairs. By now you and your family have probably realised and, hopefully, appreciated all that I did for you then.

I will never get over the hurt and devastation you caused. Even now, one year on, I cannot yet get my brain around the cruelty of what you conspired, with your brother and daughter, to do to me. I am still destroyed by the web of premeditated deceit and lies that you, Ann, Chris and probably Susan as well, tried to conceal from me. It was truly dreadful, and I do not think the scars will ever heal. You may laugh and think that you were all very clever, but I think, and maybe hope, that there is some glimmer of sorrow, remorse and shame about what you did.

So, we did not quite make 25 years of marriage, but I will still raise a glass and toast the good times we had, but now, more importantly, to what is coming next.

As close friends have said to me recently "time to close that book and open the next chapter of what life holds for me in the future".

I wish now that you would honour the divorce settlement that I agreed to accept and pay me the balance of money that is now overdue. I want nothing further to do with you, you have done me more damage than I deserve. I want now to be left to get on with my life. I will remember with fondness all the good parts of our life together, but you did not deserve all the love, devotion and care that I gave you. You repaid it with a conspiracy of lies and betrayal.

I returned home in early June with Henry, enjoying the drive back through France. Henry suggested that as Bennion was starting to get old, it might be a good time to have another puppy, whilst Bennion was fit enough to accept a new dog into the house, so I had been doing some research whilst in France. One of George's BRDC friends had a daughter whose Jack Russell had just had pups. She sent me a photo of the only one she had left for sale. He was 7 weeks old when I got back from France, so I agreed to drive over to see him. He was the fat one of the litter, he clearly had been first in the milk queue. Even that young, he had a cheeky personality and it was love at first sight. He was just gorgeous and as the vet had done all the necessary paperwork, I brought him home with me.

June 10th

And so, Basil arrived into the family. Oh, what joy he brought, poor Bennion went through the mill, Basil would swing from his ears, race round the garden and pee all over the house. Thank goodness the floors were all either marble tiles or wood!

June 24th

The next monumental episode was moving Mum and Dad to my house, tip runs, clearing out their old house and making them comfortable in my house was quite a marathon but we did it. Looking back now, it was a great thing to do, not only for them, but for me too. I had a new focus to life, it meant being disciplined again over meals and gave a structure to life, so it was a lovely time to have. Dad was by then 91 and absolutely threw himself into life in the village, joined the local Probus group, church, Mum joined "Knit and Natter and Friday Group. Dad adored Basil, spoiled him beyond reason, carried him around and had him on his knee at every opportunity. All in all, it was the beginning of a few years of fun and laughter and I will treasure that time with the "elderly's" for ever. Instead of them struggling at home by themselves, it gave them both a new lease of life and they loved it here..

I had visited George on my return from France. It was clear that the dementia was starting to take him over. He still rang me every morning without fail and every day I went to see him. He either needed to go to the Co-op for food, or the bank, or the chemist or laundry doing. I took meals down for him, made him coffee, talked to him. He was lonely and getting more and more confused. His brother came to visit when he found a reason to extract money; on one occasion George rang me to say, "Chris has taken my Jaguar". I asked why and he said that it was because he wasn't allowed to drive anymore, so he was going to sell it. He did and had the cheque for £20,000 paid into a new account in his name! Why? George was very, understandably, upset, devastated actually. Chris paid the £20,000 into George's account and then immediately stopped the cheque. George asked me for help to get the money back. The bank confirmed that the money had been paid in but then the cheque was stopped. I tried to ring the police to report this but somehow nothing was done. To this day I do not know if George ever got that money back. More dodgy dealing from his brother!! Was there no end to his scheming? Ann did not visit often as she lived in London and the money had all been redistributed, mostly to me as the divorce settlement; she wasn't going to care for her dad on a full time basis, she had her own life to lead. John came as often as he could, but he was working and had his new life with his new baby as well, so it was only once a week or so. He was a sad, lonely, confused old man, wondering what on earth had happened to his life. So, for the next few months life took on its own pattern of Mum and Dad, new puppy, and visiting and sorting George out.

August 15th

George's 70th birthday. During all the years of George's ill health, he always said that his goal would be to reach his 3 score years and 10. He said that his dad had died at 70 and he felt that he would have had a normal life span if he could achieve his aim. And he made it. So, Robert, Lindsay, Tony and I took him to the Apiary, our local wine bar, for lunch to celebrate. He was dreadfully thin, grey complexion, looking emaciated but happy to have reached his milestone. I had bought him a wool beany hat with a BRDC badge on it which he loved and wore all the time after that. He enjoyed his lunch with us all, laughed and it was a particularly good occasion. I was pleased that he was quite compos mentis with no signs of dementia that day, other than a bit of confusion.

A few weeks previously he had been really mentally ill; the cleaning ladies phoned me, very worried as they had arrived to clean for him, and he had thrown them out shouting "what are doing here. I'm in Brazil with the football team". It was when the World Cup was on and he genuinely thought he was there with the British team!

October

George was now really deteriorating, and I had him admitted back into hospital. He could not care for himself; he was getting thinner and so confused he didn't know what was what. I went to see him every other day, I was the only visitor he had other than his friend Tony, I took his pyjamas and laundry home, washed and ironed then returned to him. The consultant came to see me on one occasion and asked if I was his wife. I told him that I used to be, but we were now divorced. He said that as I had been his only visitor in 3 weeks, he wanted to talk to his next of kin, but I would suffice. He said that George's heart was failing. His original heart had almost totally stopped and the transplanted one, was very weak. He told me that George would not recover from this. I asked him the awful question "how long has he got" to which he replied that it was like predicting how long was a piece of string. At most it would be 6 months, but if he got a chest infection it would be days. Oh, how sad I felt, after the dreadful, previous year, it was almost the end. None of the trauma of 2013 should have been allowed to happen. What a sad last year of his life. I continued to visit every few days, about twice a week.

November 17th

I went to visit George as usual and to my surprise he was sat up in bed looking cheerful, shaved, hair brushed and quite chipper. "Hello Weewo" he called as I walked in. He looked better than he had done in weeks, I had taken some clean clothes in, some chocolate and jelly babies, his favourites. He said his feet were cold and would I put some socks on for him. I looked at his feet and was shocked at the state of his toenails (lovely subject). I said that they were disgraceful and when had he last cut them? He looked at me with a smile on his face and said "the last time they were done was the last time you did them for me" "but that was about 18 months ago" I said, and he nodded. Oh, dear me, how life had changed. I always did George's pedicure, kept everything nice for him. "Right, let me get these done now then" I said and persuaded the sister on duty to let me have some nail scissors and I had an emery board in my handbag. Whilst I was working on his feet, he said "I really f.....d up our marriage, didn't I?" "Yes" I replied "I was your best friend, wife, lover, nurse, business partner and you betrayed me, lied, tried to cheat me and destroyed our family. Why? What did I do to make you do that to me? I did not deserve that, did I? "No" he said," I was badly advised by my Ann and my brother, they told me that you had stolen £200,000 (remember the list of expenditure; totally gone from his brain) of our money and that you were having an affair". I said, "you knew I would never have done either of those things, I was honest and true to you all through our lives, why would I want to do that?" He said he knew deep down that I was innocent of all that and that he realised now, it was all driven by jealousy and greed. He was so sorry and wished he could take away all the sadness of the past year and a half. "You could have your old job back" he said with a big grin on his face. "Oh, and what job was that then George?" I asked. "We could get married again" he said. I looked him straight in the face and said that when he got himself better, out of hospital and back home, then we would talk about it. As I looked at him, sadly I knew that it would never happen, despite the vast improvement that evening. I knew he was never coming home again. There was no dementia that night, he was completely normal, rational, with his old sense of humour, in fact, my George of old. The sister walked past George's bed at that moment and George said to her, "I told you she'd come back to me; we are going to get married again". Sister said that she was very pleased and delighted for us both and offered her congratulations. We both looked at each other and knew it wasn't ever going to happen, but it made George happy to think so. When I left, I kissed him on top of his head and left him smiling. I just felt empty and sad. What a waste the last year or so had been.

I left with a whole pile of dirty laundry and said that it would be 2 days before I came back as I had lunch to cook for my elderly godparents, 5 x 90-year olds for lunch the following day. I kissed him goodbye and went home.

November 19th

A horrible dark, wet and cold November evening. I was so tempted to stay at home, I really didn't want to turn out to drive to the hospital, but I knew George hadn't got any more clean PJ's, so off I went. I arrived and found George in a different part of the ward. He was asleep and John was sat by the bed. It was a couple of minutes past 7pm. I talked to John, who had just returned from a 2-week holiday in Tenerife, and we just chatted in a friendly manner. I nudged George on the side of his arm and said, "are you going to wake up and talk to us, George. John wants to tell you all about his holiday?" George fluttered his eyes, not quite opened but enough for me to acknowledge that he had heard me. John and I continued to chat, quietly but easy and friendly, a few laughs about things that had happened, just general pleasant conversation, and then the nurse came in to do George's blood pressure. I said to her that he was very sleepy and not responsive, and that I'd brought clean laundry. She said that was great as she would get George ready for bed when she had done the obs. She put the cuff around George's left arm and I immediately knew from the look on her face. She asked John and I to go out of the room whilst she tried the cuff on his right arm. I just knew; he had slipped away quietly, peacefully and happily, listening to John and I chatting away. No trauma, no nastiness, just friendly chit chat. It was 7.20pm. John and I were taken to a waiting room. I couldn't cry, I was too shocked. I just shook all over. I had known that he hadn't got long for this world but didn't expect it to happen just then. I suppose, on reflection, that after our completely rational conversation 2 days before, his conscience was clear, he had apologised, he was at peace. None of Chris's histrionics and unpleasantness around; just John and I and he had simply let himself drift away.

All the years that I had sat with him, all the times he had been really ill and the times I had thought that he wouldn't make it. You would have thought that I would be prepared when it actually happened but no. I sat in the room outside tears rolling down my face, shaking all over from shock. The finality of it hit me like a train. John phoned Ann to let her know the news. He came back into the ward and looked at me, with a wry smile, and said "wow, that was a difficult one". I suspect it was because John would have told her that I was with him when he died. She would have hated that. John and I sat with George till about 9 o'clock. I took all the clean laundry back home and John took his dad's wallet, phone and other personal effects. I told John that I could phone our friends, who were funeral directors, and that I would go up to the house in the morning. Put all the laundry away, strip the bed and wash all the sheets and towels then return them so that when John and Ann were ready to clear out the house, at least everything would be clean and in order. I also told him that I was going on holiday on December 1st. He was grateful for my help as I told him that I knew exactly what George wanted, it had been discussed between us many times in the past. He said he didn't know anything so was grateful for all the help I could be. I gave him a big hug in the car park and said that it was now time to heal our fractured family. He agreed. I called into see Robert and Lindsay on the way home to tell them and had a much-needed glass of wine. Then went home to bed with a sad and heavy heart. I thought that this was the end of the whole saga. The end of nearly 27 years of life with George. The end of his suffering for 22 years of ill health. The end.

No not quite.

If anything, the final chapter of our lives together was, if anything, about to be the worst and most farcical of all.

November 20th,

I got up early as it was going to be a busy day, showered and dressed, and at 9am I was on the phone to our dear friends of many years, who were funeral directors. They have a great sense of humour and are great fun company. I suppose that in that business, a sense of humour is essential. Anyway, they were very kind, and said they would get on the case straight away. I said that I was going on holiday so wanted to get things underway immediately. I was told to leave it all to them, they would get it organised. I reminded them that as we were divorced, then Ann and John would need to give the OK and I gave them, John's phone number. 10 minutes later a phone call back gave 3 alternative dates and times at the crematorium. Having been married for so long and having gone through all the health issues with George, his funeral arrangements had been discussed between us, what music he would like, one of his oldest friends to do a eulogy etc. I knew exactly what George wanted. So, I phoned John, gave him the phone number and told him what was already in place. John thanked me and said that he was so glad that I knew what needed to be done as he didn't know where to start. I told John that I was about to go up to the house to put the laundry away and that I had a chiropractor's appointment at 11.30 so he could get hold of me after lunch. So far so good.

I went to the house; remember that George had moved into the annex and had rented out the house to tenants. Out of courtesy, I knocked on the door to tell them that George had died the night before. They said that they had already heard but thank you for coming to see us. I thought to myself, wow, news travels fast in this village!!! Anyway, up to the annex, the bed linen stripped, and the clean laundry put away. I sat down in George's armchair just to take in a few minutes' private thoughts and reflections. A few tears and great sense of sadness came over me; half of my adult life had been spent with George and despite it being stormy and rocky at times, we had enjoyed a good life together up until spring of 2013. We had gone through such a lot together, but I took comfort in the conversation we had had 2 days before he died. He was so sorry about what had happened, the rational George was back, just for a little while, and that is how I wanted to remember him; not the unpleasantness of the previous 18 months. When George had moved into the annex, he asked me if I would lend him 2 pictures, one of our wedding and the other of the 4 kids all together, as he had no family portraits to look at. I had taken them and hung them at either side of his TV so he could look at them. I took my pictures off the wall and, together with the bed linen, loaded them into the car. I looked at my watch which brought me out of my reverie and realised that it was past 10.30 and I had to get going for my back appointment. I locked up and got into the car, reversed round to drive out and at that very moment one of the tenants jumped into their car and turned around, blocking the drive. Then she jumped out and ran into the house. Damn, I thought, why has she just done that. Not thinking any other bad thoughts other than she had gone back indoors because she had forgotten something. Wrong. I went to the door to ask, very politely, if the car could be moved so I could get to my appointment. "You aren't going anywhere" a vitriolic voice came from inside. "You have been stealing and the police are on the way". "What" I replied," I've just taken the bedding to wash and put the laundry away". I wondered why I was explaining myself to the tenants. The front door was slammed and so I went back to my car wondering what the hell to do. I rang R, my lovely lawyer, for advice. "Get off the drive", she said, "lock the car and get out". So, I did, locked the car and started to walk down the drive. As I began walking, so the electronic gates started to close, so I ran and got through in the nick of time. By now it was 11am. I ran across the road to Lindsay's and asked her if she could run me into town to the chiropractors and I would explain on the way. We jumped into her car and off we went. We had not got far when my mobile phone rang; it was the police ordering me to return to the house. I was being accused of breaking and entering and theft. This was beyond belief. I tried to explain what had happened and that I was not breaking in; I had the annex keys! I had told John, not only the night before, but only about an hour and a half ago. What on earth was the problem? I told them about the tenants blocking my car on the drive and shutting the gates on me. I am still the joint owner of that property anyway as George had never bothered to do the legal transfer of ownership." I am perfectly entitled to go in and out as I please. I said that I was on my way to have my back appointment and that I would return in an hour or so when I had finished. The police said I needed to prove ownership and they would be waiting for me. I was in a total whirl; my husband had died the night before, all the horrors and trauma of the year before, everything I had been through, and now this. Think on your feet Elsie, difficult at times like this. How can I prove ownership? In a blinding flash I knew what to do. I went and had my back manipulated, I was in pain due to a fracture in my back many years before, but my muscles must have been so knotted due to stress and tension; I felt sore but better an hour later. As we started the drive home, I rang the rental agency as they had a copy of the land registry document. I asked them if they could meet me at the Key House drive with the documents which, bless their hearts, they did.

Lindsay drove the car up the hill towards the Key House and at the same moment, we both exploded with laughter and total disbelief. There were 3 police cars straddled across the drive. I said to Lindsay that I didn't think there were that many police cars at the Great Train Robbery. Lindsay pulled onto her drive opposite and asked if I wanted her to come over with me. I said "no" and that I would come over later, as long as they didn't cart me off in handcuffs!

I walked up the drive and there were 5 policemen, 1 policewoman, John, George's brother Chris, the tenants and the nosy next-door neighbours all outside the annex. I ignored them all and spoke to the policewoman. It was her that had phoned me in the car. I was furious but controlled and calm; everybody realised how angry I was. I glared at Chris; John had his head down, just as he had done in court at the divorce hearing. I said nothing, just looked. The policewoman asked why I had the keys to the annex. I said because I had a duplicate set as I was the co-owner. Chris started to object but was astonished when I proved that my name was still on the Land Registry document and also on the tenancy agreement. The policewoman asked me to prove it, so I handed her the copy of the Land Registry document and the Tenancy agreement. She said that I had been seen loading property from the annex into my car. That could only have been seen by the tenants spying on me. I told her that it was my 2 pictures and the bed linen which I had told John that I was going to wash. She told me to open my car so they could inspect the contents. I retorted "absolutely not, you are not going to rifle through my car. You have no idea of what was already in my car when I arrived. I will show you what I put into the car, but you have no right to search it". I opened the car and took out the Ikea bag that contained the sheets. With gritted teeth, I tipped the contents, a bottom fitted sheet, 2 pillowcases and a duvet cover, out onto the damp drive, in front of Chris, looking him straight in the eyes as I did it, and said to him "I've done George's laundry for the past 25 years. You can do this last load. How bloody dare you do this to me. You have interfered in my life once too often; you did not even know that I still owned the house, did you? You have wasted police time and effort. You are the liar, the cheat, who stole £20,000 from the sale of George's car and the main cause of our divorce. You are a nasty piece of work and I never want to see you ever again. You have no right even to be here. I was not breaking and entering, I had every right to be there. I told John last night and this morning what

I was doing. How bloody dare you. I've taken 2 pictures, both mine, the portrait of the 4 kids was my 40th birthday present from an old friend and the wedding portrait George had had framed for me years before, but I had lent them to George". The policewoman started to realise that this was all nonsense, a complete waste of police time and merely a domestic situation, but she had to keep up the charade to save her face. She asked me to open the house and asked John to check through to make sure that nothing else was missing. Well of course he had not got a clue as he didn't know. I walked with John into the house and out of earshot of all the others I turned around to him, looked him straight in the face and said "John, you should be ashamed of this. After sitting with you and your dad last night, saying that it was time to heal our fractured family, giving him a big hug, telling him what I was doing this morning. What were you thinking, I only spoke to you 2 hours ago on the phone? This is a complete farce, waste of police time, just sheer stupidity" John said nothing, there wasn't much he could say really. We locked up the house, the policewoman wanted me to hand over the keys to the annex and I refused as it was still my property. She made me put the pictures back in the house, which was futile anyway as I retrieved them later. Then the police started to pack up to leave. I said "Right, if there's nothing else, we are finished here, and I am going to go home. John, Chris, neighbours, all of you, get off my property - now." To the tenants, "it was not a good idea to block the legal owner of the house, your landlord now, from leaving my own drive, was it? I will be legally informing you of notice to quit. You have 2 months to pack up and get out. If you do not leave the property in good, clean order, the deposit will not be refunded as in the rental contract terms." To the police I said," I will be expecting a written apology from yourselves for not checking your facts before you came here, for your attitude in my time of grief and I hope that you will be charging Chris for gross waste of police time". Summoning all my dignity, and standing as tall as I could, I got into my car and drove down the drive, only to find my daughter Alison at the bottom. "Mum, are you ok?" She cried. "Yes, I am fine, go across to Lindsay's, I need coffee, and right now". I said.

Alison, by then pregnant with baby Amelia, had driven over to see me after my earlier phone call to tell her about George's death. She had arrived, only to be told by Mum and Dad about what was going on at the Key House, as of course, I had kept them informed. Alison drove straight down to see what she could do to help. What a storm in a teacup! An absolute fiasco. Just unbelievable.

We both went into Lindsay's together. I retained my sense of indignation, fury, total disbelief and incredulity till I got into Lindsay's. Bless her and Alison. I would have collapsed in floods of tears if I had been alone, the absolute b…..d's, but they both lifted me and made me laugh at the sheer debacle I had just experienced. We had coffee, then wine and discussed the events of the morning. It was beyond belief and I was struggling to comprehend what I had just gone through, so unbelievable. I could only shake my head in total stupefaction. How does anyone make any sense of that morning? If it wasn't all so sad you could almost laugh. The phrase "you couldn't make it up" comes to mind. The reality was though, that I had just lived through it. Like an event in a Reality TV Show. Completely cruel, unnecessary, stupid, words fail me to make any sense of it and in my moment of grief over the death of my husband of all those years. Tell me how to get my head around that?

Obviously, after he had gone home from the hospital the night before, John had rung Chris to tell him the news. John, I imagine, must have told Chris that I was going up to the house to take the clean laundry back so then Chris had taken it upon himself to ring the tenants, to tell them to stop me leaving and had called the police saying that I had been caught breaking and entering. Chris had then driven down from Yorkshire to witness the debacle. What was he trying to achieve? A moment of triumph or revenge? What a performance. Such a drama and complete nonsense. What was in Chris's brain? What had I ever done to him to make him hate me so much other than to have thwarted his plan to disinherit me? Continuing to interfere, as he had been doing for the past couple of years but without knowing the true facts. How absolutely stupid, what an absolute idiot he had made of himself, yet again! I still to this day don't know what I ever did to make him, and Ann hate me so much. Just jealousy and greed I think.

After George and I had made our peace 2 days before he died, he would have been beyond distressed at this display yet again, engineered by his brother Chris.

Alison and I went back home, still in a state of disbelief. The final straw to the day was the funeral director ringing me back saying "so very sorry Elsie but all the dates offered have been rejected and we have been instructed that that we hold the funeral when you are away on holiday. I have said that I thought it was very unkind as you guys had been married for such a long time, but those are my instructions.

I can't tell you how sad I am". It is beyond anything we have ever encountered. I said that I was really not surprised as they had not had the pleasure of meeting my ex family before!.

It was an act of such monumental cruelty that I can never forget or forgive.

THE END

And so, it was, the funeral was booked for Wednesday 3rd December, knowing that I would have departed for my holiday to Egypt with 5 friends on Monday 1st December.

November 27th would have been the 17th anniversary of George's Heart Transplant. I decided that as I would not be at the funeral, I would hold a celebration of the fact that George had had 17 years of bonus. I rang and emailed all our friends, saying that this was absolutely not an alternative funeral but a celebration of George's life. I said that I would be at the John Thompson Inn from 12 noon on 27th November. Anyone who would care to come for a drink with me would be very welcome. I had George's racing videos playing on the screen, not sure if anyone would turn up. I put £100 behind the bar for anyone to have a drink but did not know who might come. By 2pm the pub was full to exploding. I put another £200 behind the bar and I was astonished, touched and tearful. So many came, George's BRDC friends, my Doghouse Ladies, Round Table and 41 club friends, neighbours, just over 200 people. The owner and his wife produced food from nowhere and we did not get home till nearly 5pm. I was never charged for excess drinks or buffet, they just said it was their pleasure to do this for me. Everyone was disgusted at what had gone on during the last couple of years and were horrified for what had been done. I just had a toast to George, to 17 years of his transplant, a thank you to Harefield Hospital for giving him that, to the young man who had donated his heart and we all wished that George would find a Racetrack in Heaven.

3rd December, In Egypt, in my cabin on the Nile, my brother, 4 friends and I had a bottle of Champagne to mark the time of the actual funeral taking place back home. It was a very, very difficult moment for me but so very glad and grateful that I had my close friends around to support me.

George's funeral went ahead, with nothing that George had wanted, because his family did not know what he had planned, and they did not have the courtesy to ask me what he did want. His wife (me) of 25 years was not there. I was the "elephant in the room" as his friends said to me afterwards, his stepson, David and stepdaughter, Alison, were not there, his mother and father in law, (my parents) were not there and lots of his friends were not there, having chosen to come to the Celebration of Life as a mark of support for me and disgust of his family. How sad. How incredibly sad. How petty minded. How selfish. How cruel. Just summed up the attitude of his family.

George would have been furious that his funeral didn't take place as he had wanted, he would have been devastated that I had been deliberately excluded. His choices of music; "Lady in Red", (on our first proper dinner date, I wore a red, off the shoulder dress and it was a favourite dress and song of ours thereafter), "Hotel California", by the Eagles and Elvis, "It's Now or Never" were not played, his eulogy should have been delivered by a lifelong racing friend, which didn't happen. The collection was sent to the British Heart Foundation and, whilst that is a very worthwhile charity, George wanted any donations to go to Harefield Transplant Unit. All because his family chose to deny me the opportunity of advising of his wishes and being there. After all those years of love, care and total devotion. At least I know in my heart that George had made his peace with me, he realised what he had done and had apologised so his conscience was clear when he died.

EPILOGUE

Well this book has taken an exceptionally long time to write, over 20 years in total. It started out as an account of the story of George's Heart Transplant. A story that was remarkable in itself. It was just meant to be a diary leading up to the surgery but as time went on there was just so much more to tell.

Just to bring all of this together, it is now September 2020. We have all been in lockdown due to the Corona Virus, Covid 19. Now, being unable to go out has given me the final impetus to finish my book and I feel a huge sense of relief that I have got to the end of the saga. From start to finish it has been a catharsis for me to write it and now I feel I can start my life all over again, despite reaching the vast age of 70 last November. The trauma of it all has taken its' toll on me and damaged me. I cannot ever forget, but at least I have written it all down, it is now recorded as it was. Every word I have written is true, no embellishment and no fantasy, although there are many other aspects that I could have added but, in retrospect, are best left unsaid. The writing of it has, at times been exceedingly difficult, especially 2013, but in many ways, I feel relieved, set free, I can breathe again, live and hopefully love again, sing and dance. Whether I will ever be able to trust completely again remains to be seen. I have survived, I am OK. I feel as if I have carried a huge weight on me for many years. So many emotions, so many tears shed. Sometimes I felt the victim, but I know that they would have succeeded if I allowed myself to feel that. I am not a victim; I am a survivor. Where all the strength came from, I do not know; I am not unscathed, but I am OK.

There is no moral to the story but maybe a few pointers for anyone going through similar circumstances. When you care for a loved one going through some serious health issues be prepared for some dramatic changes in behaviour. Side effects from tablets can affect mood and temperament, fear of the future, anger and pain can affect the way people react towards their nearest and dearest. Jealousy, in that the person you love is in good health whilst you are not, is a natural reaction, though all these facets can be incredibly difficult to live with. Patience is a great asset. Talk to each other, communication is absolutely vital and understanding of each other. It is so much better for all concerned if the whole family can come together to support, not only the one who is sick but importantly to help and support the carer who is living with the sufferer 24 hours of every day, 365 days of the year. Conflict within the family is just so destructive. Money is (I do not know who originally said it) the root of all evil. Well I am not sure about that, but it can certainly bring out the worst in people. I am not the first, nor will I be the last, to be at the centre of disputes over inheritance in families. Greed is regarded as one of the Seven Deadly Sins and for good reason. In a fair and proper world, we should all be able to trust one another. Sadly, we are not perfect, and my trust has been irreparably lost. I will from now on trust myself and my own judgement. Maybe a sad indictment, but I have learned through experience to look after myself first and never again become complacent.

I will laugh, I will enjoy, I will treasure every moment from now on. Life is for living now, it is not a rehearsal.

Who knows what life has in store for, hopefully, my next 20 years, if I should be so lucky? Hopefully, I can find love again. No more lies, ever. Lots of happiness and laughter in my future life and maybe even trust. Please, though, no more curved balls!

POSTSCRIPT

September 2020

Dad died in 2017 aged 93,

Mum is now 93 and living in a wonderful care home and as fit as a fiddle, with no dementia, thank goodness, staying safe from Covid 19

Alison and Carl are the parents of the most delightful and gorgeous Amelia, my granddaughter, now aged 5.

David, sadly just been made redundant. Like so many others a result of the current Covid 19 pandemic crisis. I am desperately hoping he will soon find a new career.

I am still living at Home Farm Courtyard, in the lovely barn conversion I bought after the divorce, though in isolation at the moment.

Chris died a couple of years ago. I can't speak ill of the dead but, I have no grief for him.

The names of all the characters in this story have been changed to protect the real identities of the family, but every word I have written is a true tale. Those of my family and friends who lived through this with me will know who is who. They know that what I have said is the absolute truth.

I am sad about the loss of my relationship with John, I always loved him but the only way I can cope with all of this is to obliterate George's family from my head. It is to this day, too painful to have them as part of my life. They have done too much damage to me, my daughter and son. Our family was just torn apart and no amount of glue can ever stick it back together. I just wish him and his family well for the future.

I have no feelings of bitterness. It is pointless and just eats you up inside and damages you further.

I just carry a huge sadness that it happened. With family support and help, it could have ended very differently, but it did not, because of greed, jealousy and lies.

I am so lucky, despite everything that happened, I survived and still am able to enjoy

LIFE – THE ULTIMATE GIFT

Lightning Source UK Ltd.
Milton Keynes UK
UKHW010634031120
372717UK00001B/187